How to Create a Successful
Adoption Portfolio

Easy Steps to Help You
Produce the Best Adoption Profile
and Prospective Birthparent Letter

Madeleine Melcher

Jessica Kingsley *Publishers*
London and Philadelphia

First published in 2014
by Jessica Kingsley Publishers
73 Collier Street
London N1 9BE, UK
and
400 Market Street, Suite 400
Philadelphia, PA 19106, USA

www.jkp.com

Library of Congress Cataloging in Publication Data
Melcher, Madeleine.
  How to create a successful adoption portfolio : easy steps to help you produce the best adoption profile and prospective birthparent letter / Madeleine Melcher.
    pages cm
  ISBN 978-1-84905-946-6
  1. Adoptive parents. 2. Adoption. 3. Birthmothers. 4. Birthparents. I. Title.
  HV875.M3957 2014
  362.734--dc23
                                2013036956

British Library Cataloguing in Publication Data
A CIP catalogue record for this book is available from the British Library

ISBN 978 1 84905 946 6
eISBN 978 0 85700 764 3

Printed and bound in the United States

For my mother, Elizabeth Dees Noll, who loved me with all her heart without a thought to biology and always wanted me to write a book. For my husband Phil, who held me up with his faith and love, as we went through our three adoptions and who has made it possible for me to follow my dreams. For my children, my blessings, my joys—Philip, Elizabeth and Noah, I could not love you more. For my sister Anna, who will be my forever friend by choice. For Peggy, my first editor, who has believed in me and lifted me up with the joy she has for all that my children do. For all birthmothers, who are truly where an adoption story begins. And for all the adoptive parents who have allowed me to be a part of their journeys; it has been one of my life's great honors.

A special thanks also to those who have given me permissions to use their works as a part of samples for this book or allowed me to speak with them for insight and additional information.

Contents

1

Introduction

I understand…

When you are seeking to adopt a child, after filling out what seems to be endless paperwork, completing your home study, undergoing background checks, providing fingerprints and attending parenting classes, you are given what is likely to be your biggest task of all.

The adoption portfolio you are told to create is one of the most important tools on which your future hopes of building a family are relying. The amount of direction given by adoption agencies or attorneys varies; some clients I have worked with were given no guidelines and left to "wing it," while others have pages and pages of specific and somewhat tedious guidelines. Maybe you fall somewhere in between. Whatever the case may be, like anything important that you do, you should know as much as possible about it before diving in.

I've been where you are right now…feeling hopeful and excited, while also overwhelmed and confused, wondering where to begin with your adoption portfolio/profile. I understand the boat you are in. Having been adopted in Germany as a 14-month-old myself, I always had plans to adopt at some point, but when I could not get pregnant after two years of fertility treatments, my husband and I decided that what we really wanted was a baby. By that point I would have taken a purple alien baby; I just wanted a baby. We chose an agency and completed all of our paperwork. When we attended our orientations at the adoption agency office, we were introduced to the requirement of a "birthmother letter." As I listened to our adoption advisor explain exact size specifications and information sections that had to be included, my mind was spinning. Never mind the fact that they wanted one-hundred handmade copies. Our hopes of being chosen for a child hinged on just a few pieces a paper. What would I fill them with, that would persuade someone to choose us to love and raise their child? Did I have the words? What colors would I use? What did the prospective birthparents really want to know? HELP!

Things have changed since that first birthmother letter I created; most agencies now require full portfolios rather than just a letter and we have gone on to adopt three children in less time than I could have carried any of them myself. It is also no longer appropriate to refer to what you create as a birthmother letter, because the expectant mother is not really a birthmother until she actually places her child with a family through adoption. What has not changed since my first adoption is that the letter or portfolio you create is what prospective birthparents will use to decide if you are further considered or chosen as the family for their child. Before you start worrying more about your portfolio, remember, YOU KNOW THE ANSWERS—YOUR PORTFOLIO IS ABOUT YOU! What you might not know is what you should include about yourselves, how to choose pictures that truly tell your story and how best to lay out and embellish your pages—that is what I am here for!

It never occurred to me that others needed help with their portfolios/profiles until our adoption agency called me after our second adoption, and asked if I could help some of their other families with their portfolios. I will always be thankful to our agency representative Susan, not just for guiding us to two of our three children but for suggesting I help others on the journey to theirs. When I first started creating custom portfolios and was working primarily with clients from Susan's agency, she often referred to them as "magical," as they were always chosen so quickly. I have been creating adoption portfolios for prospective adoptive parents all over the United States since 2005. I have been fortunate to see some of my clients chosen by prospective birthmothers, based solely on their portfolios, within a week or less of the portfolio's completion. It is my hope that this book will give you the help you need as you create your portfolio and follow your own journey to the child that is meant to be yours.

I have worked to provide you with answers from experienced adoption attorneys and adoption agency directors, insight into what is important to prospective birthmothers and how it relates to your portfolio, guidance in composing your text and an overview of layout and design. The samples I have provided use real client photos (with permission), not a batch of professionally created pictures. None of the samples you will see in this book require advanced knowledge of cutting free-form pictures and other advanced design skills, as I may use for a portfolio I design, but are doable for anyone. I want you to know what to do and where to get what you need to do it, but also to know that you CAN do it!

2

What is an Adoption Portfolio or Adoption Profile?

You will find the most important tool you will have in your adoption journey has many names: adoption portfolio, adoption profile, family profile, parent profile and family résumé, just to name a few. Whatever name you choose to go with, your portfolio is basically a snapshot of your life and the life you are offering the prospective birthparents' child. Adoption portfolios are used by most adoption agencies, adoption attorneys, and those who are seeking adoption independently to market to expectant parents who are considering adoption as a plan for their child. The expectant parents are often looking at four or more portfolios at a time, which means yours must stand out from the rest if you want to get a second look. Your portfolio is your first impression and sometimes your only impression. Many times, prospective birthparents would prefer to choose a family from a stack of portfolios than to narrow down portfolios and then meet with those families. Knowing that your portfolio may be your only "contact" with a prospective birthmother, you will want to make your *best* impression, right from the start.

Don't let the blank page stop you…

The word I hear most often when I speak to new clients is "overwhelmed." The enormity and importance of the final product can leave prospective adoptive parents stressed and suffering from a creative block before they even begin. While there is a lot to do, there is actually very little over which prospective adoptive parents have control, as they make their attempt to successfully adopt a child. You can make known your preferences of race, exposure and cost involved with your adoption. You may eventually be able to decide whether or not you would like to match with a prospective birthfamily that would like to match with you, but beyond that, your portfolio is the only part of the process you truly have control over. From start to finish, you decide how prospective birthparents will see you and ultimately that will play one of the biggest parts in whether you are matched or not. Do not let the process of creating your portfolio be something to dread, instead look at it as a chance to play an important role in your adoption.

Whether you chose this guide because you wanted to know what questions prospective birthmothers have, or to give you an idea of where to start with layout resources or text elements you should choose, you will find direction here. Along with your agency or attorney guidelines, it will help you get this done! Because it is a likely requirement to have your portfolio completed in order to be shown to prospective birthparents, do not put this off! Most agencies will allow your portfolio to be shown as soon as your home study is complete. To put off creating your portfolio is to create missed opportunities. The sooner you successfully complete your portfolio, the sooner you can be presented.

3

Before You Do Anything Else

The first place you need to look

The first thing you should do before you do anything else is to look at any and all guidelines you have been given by your adoption agency or adoption attorney. The portfolio guidelines I see when I work with my clients can vary from very strict, four-page guidelines to almost no guidelines, and everything in between. It is important to know what your agency or attorney wants and to follow their requests. There are a number of agencies who will not allow your portfolio to be shown until they have given it their approval. It can only help you to be sure your portfolio is done to their specifications the first time. This is also why, if you have not yet chosen an agency or attorney with whom to work, you will not want to do more than to think about text and gather some pictures until you have decided on an agency and have their guidelines in hand. It would be terrible to go through all the work entailed in a portfolio, only to find it does not meet the specific guidelines of the agency or attorney you end up working with.

When looking at your guidelines:

- Note whether they specify portrait or landscape design.

- Be clear about how many pages, minimum and maximum, are required.

- Make an outline of the pages or topics your agency or attorney has required (if you are left to choose your own, there is a suggested list in the Portfolio Workbook section of this book).

- Think about how your life relates to the topics and the pictures you will need for each one.

- Get your camera ready. If you are short on pictures relating to the topics that are required, keep your camera with you from now on and take all the shots you can.

- Know whether they want you to include a "tag line" with their contact information on it.

- Be sure of any restrictions regarding how your portfolio layout is designed (by hand, digitally, by a designer).

- Understand what kind of printing and binding is required for your portfolio, as well as how many copies your agency or attorney would like from you.

As you look at the guidelines, you will want to be clear about any and all of the requirements of your agency or attorney. Becoming acquainted with your agency or attorney expectations will save you time and headaches in the long run. If you have any questions at all about what they are seeking from you, ask them as soon as you possibly can. Your agency or attorney wants to see you succeed, and, while they cannot always get back to you immediately, they do want to help you. This book can guide you through what you need to know to create a portfolio, but before you start putting things together you must know the specifics your agency or attorney is requiring of you.

What you need to know about your reader

Before we go any further with "how-tos" or lists of things to consider including, I want to be sure you have not fallen into the trap of creating your portfolio with an imaginary prospective birthmother in mind. The biggest problem for prospective adoptive parents is not their forgetting to direct their portfolio to the "audience," it is overly directing it to an imaginary audience. Your portfolio is more about your letting the prospective birthparent or birthparents get to know you and what you have to offer, than it is about making assumptions about the expectant mother and who she is or what she feels. That said, there are many people who make false assumptions or generalizations about expectant mothers who are considering an adoption plan or those birthmothers who have already placed a child with an adoptive family. One of the best things you can do, as you prepare your portfolio and perhaps go on to speak with or share a relationship with these expectant mothers, is to gain a better understanding of the truths about them. Accepting that many of the things you have heard about these women are untrue or do not fit the majority of prospective birthmothers can only benefit you as you make your adoption journey.

Marian Huet, Adoption Services Director at Love and Hope Adoptions, wants to help dispel the many myths that surround the expectant mothers and birthmothers that play a leading role in the adoption process. In her years as an adoption professional, Marian has been fortunate to know many of these women:

Birthmothers are women who are the most selfless loving individuals that anyone could ever meet. They are women who are sacrificing their genuine love toward their child to provide him or her with a better life. Birthmothers have bravely chosen to not terminate their pregnancy. Yet they will be branded by our society for placing their child with an adoptive family and their bravery will often go unrecognized.

These are women of great character and strength. They have chosen to face and travel through the storm that will come at them because of others who do not understand the gift and love that is adoption. Birthmothers do not choose the easy way of abortion so that their days can appear the same in the eyes of others; so that they do not have to provide explanations. They will carry their child for nine months in selfless sacrifice while trying not to bond further, trying not to fall in love deeper, trying to not picture his or her face.

These women have eternal courage for they will have to daily and for the rest of their lives deny their desire to parent their child. As the years pass they still remember and feel the same eternal love. They are accepting of another woman who will be called mom. They understand that another will wipe their child's tears away. The other woman will receive the hugs and the praise but the birthmother always remembers, in her undying love, that this is the most selfless choice for her child.

Every woman who places her child in the arms of another for adoption is unique and wonderful. Every birthmother has traveled a different road which led her to the choice of adoption. Some are married. Many are students. Some have been raped. Others were lied to, used, and left pregnant by the men they loved and trusted. Many have families who disown them. Anyone whose life has been touched by a birthmother has experienced true love without measure.

There are many myths about (prospective) birthmothers and accepting them as truths can lead you astray as you create your portfolio. I think it is important that you know the truths so that you can begin the process and your portfolio without misconception.

Common myths about (prospective) birthmothers

Myth # 1: They are all teenagers.

Truth # 1: Birthmothers ages can range from the teen years to sometimes near 40 years of age. Different life circumstances lead women of all ages to consider an adoption plan for the child they are carrying, so to direct your portfolio only to the teenage birthmother would be a mistake. I have seen prospective adoptive parents attempt to design their portfolio with the interests and visual preferences they think a teenager would have in mind. Those families are not only overlooking much of their audience, but they are also missing the purpose of the portfolio, which is to express themselves and convey a feeling of their own family and what they have to offer to the prospective birthmother or birthfamily.

Myth # 2: All birthmothers got pregnant because they were careless and having unprotected sex.

Truth # 2: There are a number of birthmothers who were using some form of birth control that failed or their life circumstances changed after they were already pregnant. How prospective birthmothers came to find themselves pregnant and considering an adoption plan is not ours to judge, nor really any of our business as prospective adoptive parents.

Myth # 3: The birthmothers chose adoption over abortion.

Truth # 3: "Untrue; for many of us, abortion was never an option. Abortion is seen as a reproductive choice and adoption is a parenting choice." (Coley Strickland, birthmother and co-founder of BirthMom Buds.)

Myth # 4: If they truly loved their babies they would not be able to give them up. Birthparents do not want or love their babies.

Truth # 4: "This is so untrue and probably the most hurtful misconception of all. There is a big difference between an unplanned pregnancy and an unwanted pregnancy. Just because we were not planning to get pregnant does not mean that we didn't want or love our child. The minute we found out we were pregnant, unplanned as it may have been, our children were loved and wanted." (Coley Strickland, birthmother and co-founder of BirthMom Buds.)

There is no doubt that most prospective birthparents love the children they are considering placing. There are some expectant mothers who try not to feel a deep connection to their unborn child because it is too hard knowing they cannot parent the child after birth. No matter the level of feeling they allow themselves, their baby is important enough to them to make the choice to give them a life with another family. This choice cannot be overlooked. It is not ours to judge if the feelings they have for their child are "enough" to us, nor to put what would be our own feelings on them. When writing your text directly to the prospective birthmother or birthfamily, it may come easy to write things like, "We *know* this is…" You in fact do *not* know what she is feeling or what she will feel down the road. Assumptions should never be made about her feelings or the life she has or will know.

> *Myth # 5:* Prospective birthmothers/birthfamilies are looking for the perfect family.

> *Truth # 5:* You may be worried that you are not the perfect family, with the biggest house, most impressive occupations and largest bank accounts…don't. *Prospective birthmothers are not looking for the perfect prospective adoptive family, but the perfect family for their child.* What makes the best family can mean different things to different prospective birthmothers. For some it means you have a large extended family, for others it may mean you enjoy weekly family game nights. When you put your portfolio together it is most important not that you try to be the perfect family, but that you be yourself. You don't know what will appeal to each individual prospective birthparent and even if you did, you cannot be someone you are not. This is the time to be genuine. This is the time to be yourself. When you create your portfolio, keep in mind that it is the funny stories, special traditions and unique details of your life that will make you stand out from other prospective adoptive families and lead you to the prospective birthmother or birthfamily you are meant to match with.

Adoption Attorney, Jennifer Fairfax, assists prospective birthmothers and adoptive parents every day and makes it very clear that honesty and being yourself can go a long way.

> I have represented birthparents for over 15 years. In every case, parents made a loving choice that they felt was in the best interest of their child. Birthparents range in age from young teenagers to forty and represent the full spectrum of backgrounds and financial situations: un- and fully-employed; medically/mentally-challenged and healthy; homeless and secure living arrangements. Because so much is unknown (by the prospective birthparents) about the prospective adoptive parent(s), I always advise my clients to be themselves as they prepare their profiles/portfolios; to be open, honest and transparent; to never assume anything about the woman or man who may be reading the profile or to try to "market" to a particular type of birthparent. The ultimate quest is to find a family who will provide a safe and loving environment for their child. So the portfolio/profile should be authentic, reflecting your true self. Doing so will avoid surprises and/or disappointment when the parties meet, which is how both sets of parents want to start an adoption plan.

Myth # 6: Prospective birthparents want information about the potential adoptive parents so that they can track the child down later on.

Truth # 6: Prospective birthparents want information about the potential adoptive parents in order to feel comfortable with their decision to place their child with a particular family. According to Angie Flannery from the Community Adoption Center, what prospective birthparents are looking for is peace of mind and to see that their child is loved and well cared for. They do not want to overstep boundaries, but they often do want to be able to connect with the adoptive parents to receive updates and photos of their child.

Myth # 7: Birthmothers come from a troubled past and that is why they chose adoption.

Truth # 7: "While some birthmothers have had struggles, many birthmothers are working or attending school/college and some are even raising children already. They have thought through their options with an unplanned pregnancy and want to give their unborn child a chance to have more than she may be able to give him/her." (Angie Flannery from the Community Adoption Center).

Myth # 8: Birthmothers will move on and forget about their child.

Truth # 8: "This is untrue as giving birth is a life changing experience. We instantly fall in love with our baby and we will never 'move on.' We will move forward and try to have a happy and productive life but we will never ever forget about our child. Some days are harder than others; holidays, birthdays, and Mother's Day remind us that a piece of our heart is missing." (Coley Strickland, birthmother and co-founder of BirthMom Buds).

Myth # 9: Birthmothers' children are a gift that they are giving the adoptive parents.

Truth # 9: "While you, the prospective adoptive parents, may see it this way, this is untrue in a birthmother's heart and mind. We see it as you, the adoptive parents, are the gift we are giving our children since we feel that you are more equipped to give them the things they need that we cannot provide at that time in our lives." (Coley Strickland, Birthmother and co-founder of BirthMom Buds).

4

What Prospective Birthmothers are Looking for

What do you write to people you do not know, but who will decide whether you are blessed with a child or not? It may seem like a lot of pressure, but, in fact, you have all the answers. It is all about you! Just like every human being, birthparents are all different, with differing backgrounds, preferences, styles, and life views. That said, there are very clear elements that most birthparents will be looking for as they choose a family for their child. Do not lose sight of the fact that the portfolio is about you and you are not to gear it towards a specific type of prospective birthparent you have imagined in your head. Instead, keep in mind what elements of your life will be important to most, if not all, prospective birthparents and be sure to include them in your pictures and text.

The questions a prospective birthparent has about you are many of the questions you may have asked yourself before deciding you were ready to grow your family:

- Are you emotionally ready?

- Are you financially stable?

- How does your family feel about your adoption plan?

- Will you provide for a child's education?

- What childcare plan will you make once a child is in your home?

These are core questions to which prospective birthparents will look for answers; everything else you add to your portfolio will be what sets you apart. What makes your family unique may become the reason a birthparent chooses you to parent their child. A birthparent counselor once told me that a birthmother chose a family because the family raised rabbits. Am I suggesting you go out and buy some rabbits? No. But I do suggest you be yourself. There will be a birthmother who is as right for you as you are right for her.

Many of my clients ask if they can change their portfolio for specific birthparents. The answer is no. Why? Because birthparents may each be different, but your family is a constant. What you write and create in your portfolio is about you. You cannot change yourself or be something you are not, in order to cater to specific prospective birthparents. It is the job of your agency or attorney to decide what families are best to show a particular potential birthparent. Do not try to be what you think they want you to be: Be the best of you!

Angie Flannery and her staff at the Community Adoption Center are clear on the importance of prospective adoptive parents being themselves. They suggest, as I have, that when creating your profile, you don't try to show yourselves as the people you *think* the prospective birthparent wants to see. Being genuine and offering true and meaningful information about yourselves is what a birthparent will connect with and appreciate. Angie notes that often the prospective birthparents are looking for one or more common things: to see a part of themselves, something they lacked growing up, or things they are unable to provide.

Examples of this, as seen firsthand by Angie at the Community Adoption Center:

> One family wrote in their profile that they believed their family would be wonderful and accepting of any child. The birthmother, being from a smaller, less diverse town so appreciated that they used the word 'accepting' because she knew her community was not very accepting. Another birthmother wanted to be a teacher when she was older. Both adoptive parents were teachers, and she felt a connection to that.

I cannot say it enough: You do not have to be perfect; you just need to be the perfect choice for one prospective birthmother!

Out of the mouths of BirthMoms

So what is important to expectant mothers who are choosing a family with whom to place their child and how does it relate to your portfolio text and pictures? Before I begin telling you how you can lay out your portfolio design or give you any examples of portfolio pages, I think it is most important for you to know what core ingredients your audience is looking for. You will in no way be altering who your family truly is, based on this information. Your main objective in creating your adoption portfolio is to let prospective birthparents know about you and the life you are offering their child, so it is important to know what it is that most prospective birthparents want to know about you.

In my work as an adoption portfolio designer, I have had the privilege to speak with numerous prospective adoptive parents, adoption agency social workers, and birthmothers. I think that the people who really become lost in the equation can be the prospective birthmothers. I think it is so beneficial from the start that prospective adoptive parents understand the place these women are coming from; it will only stand to help you with your portfolio and at every stage of the process.

One birthmother, in particular, has the ear of countless others. Nicole "Coley" Strickland became a birthmother in 2001 when she gave birth to her son, Charlie, and entrusted him to his adoptive family three days after his birth.

> I wasn't really prepared for the emotions I would experience after Charlie's birth and relinquishment. Grieving and sleepless one night a few weeks after Charlie's birth, I turned on my computer and began typing adoption related words into my search engine longing for another birthmother to talk to. After a lot of searching, I stumbled upon an 'Is anyone out there' post by another birthmother named LeiLani. She had placed her baby just four days before Charlie was born. We began talking and quickly became close friends. When our kids were around a year old, we began to discuss the idea of creating a central haven for birthmothers to go to and find support thus BirthMom Buds, a website and support organization for birthmothers and pregnant women considering adoption, was born. Since founding BirthMom Buds, I have become very active in the adoption community sharing my personal story and the mission of BirthMom Buds with others through speaking, newspaper and magazine interviews, and radio talk shows. I have had the privilege of meeting and working with many expectant mothers making adoption plans and birthmothers from all over the United States.

At any given time, BirthMom Buds has a network of over 900 birthmothers from all over the United States, as well as several other countries. The women in their network may be at any point of the adoption process, from an expectant mother considering an adoption plan to a birthmother who has already placed her child.

"Choosing A Family": What BirthMoms are asked to consider and what it means to you

The following extracts from "Choosing a Family" are taken with permission from www. BirthMomBuds.com. "Choosing a Family" was created by BirthMom Buds to help expectant mothers through the process of choosing a family, but it can also give you a small glimpse into what a prospective birthparent may be thinking about as they make these important decisions. Beneath each segment from the BirthMom Buds Tips and Questions you will find my comments regarding how these issues may relate to you as prospective adoptive parents and how they should be addressed, if at all, in your portfolio.

BIRTHMOM BUDS' "CHOOSING A FAMILY"

In today's era of adoptions, an expectant mom making an adoption plan is able to choose the adoptive parents who will raise her child. Choosing a family can be overwhelming and confusing at times. Before you begin that process, it is helpful to think about what characteristics you would like the family to have. Sometimes expectant mothers look for families that have similar qualities to their own families. They might also look for families that have qualities that their family lacked and they might have often wished for while growing up, depending on whether or not they had a happy childhood.

Typically, and especially if you are working with an adoption agency, you will first be given some profiles of hopeful parents to browse. These profiles usually include a letter from the prospective adoptive parents to you, photos, and general information about them that will give you a glimpse of who they are. When you are ready, you will have the capability to contact them either directly or through your agency, and ultimately arrange a time to meet them in person.

While prospective birthparents have the capability to meet and speak with you after seeing your adoption portfolio, not all of them will want to. Some prospective birthparents would prefer to choose a family based solely on their portfolio. Some will want only to speak on the phone, while other prospective birthparents will want to meet with you face to face and may want a continued relationship either until their child's birth or beyond.

A few things to think about before you begin searching for a family to raise your baby:

- What is my vision of how open I want my adoption plan to be?

    In order for your adoption plan to be successful, you need to choose an adoptive family that has the same or similar vision of an adoption plan. Think of the type and amount of contact you would like and then look for families that have similar desires.

You may not yet have a vision of an adoption plan that would be amenable to you. Your idea of the kind of contact you would like with a birthfamily may also change with time, depending on the birthparent with which you ultimately match. While these are things about which you should be thinking, do not feel you have to "lock in" on an answer now. Nor does this have to be something you include in your portfolio.

- How important to me is it that my baby be raised in a two parent family?

  For some moms, not being able to provide a stable father is one of the main reasons for placing their baby with an adoptive family. But for others, a single parent placement may be suitable if the parent can completely provide for the child. Please keep in mind that adoptive families are not immune to divorce. Just because you choose a two parent family does not mean that it will always be a two parent family.

If you are a single person who is pursuing adoption, obviously you are not going to run out and get married to meet the requirements of those expectant mothers that would prefer a two parent family. There are things you can highlight in your portfolio to help show prospective birthparents that you can provide a suitable home without a second parent. (See the section How to write text as a single prospective parent, in Chapter 7). As for married couples, it is important to stress the strengths and stability of your relationship.

- Is it important to me that my baby have a stay at home parent?

  Again for some moms choosing adoption, this may be very important to them as it is another thing they cannot give their children. For others, a stay at home parent is not quite as important. Some birthmoms may have longed for a stay at home mom growing up and may want their child to have a stay at home mom. Again, keep in mind that things change and the mom may eventually need or choose to go back to work.

Being a stay-at-home parent may not be an option for your family, and that is OK. As stated above, it may not be as important to some prospective birthparents that a parent stays at home. If you are going to have a stay-at-home parent, once a child has been placed with your family, then by all means put that information in your portfolio and fully describe all the positives and experiences you will share in that capacity. If you are a family who will have two working parents, you can stress the advantages of having two incomes, while explaining the flexibility you have in your chosen occupation and the priority you still give to your family.

- Do I want my baby to be an only child or do I want him or her to have siblings?

  An adoptive family could have plans to adopt another child after yours and then for a myriad of reasons it might not happen. They might be planning to have just one child and then circumstances could change. But there are some birthmoms who want to place their child with a family who does not have any children yet, maybe because they were the first and they want their child to be the first too. Yet to other birthmoms this might not be as important. A birthmom who had older brothers or sisters or wished for them may want her child placed with a family that already has children.

Whether you are a couple who does not have any children yet or you are a family of four already, you are who you are. There are some prospective birthparents who really do want their child to be the first and "get all the attention" and there are plenty of couples who have no children that can fill this role. For prospective adoptive families with children, either biological or adopted, there are certainly positives you can include that may even appeal to an expectant mother who had thought she would want a couple with no children. (In Chapter 7 there is a full section relating to this, Biological children in the home, and also in Chapter 6.)

- Is religion a factor?

  For some birthmoms religion is very important. If you were raised a devout Catholic, it might be important to you that your baby be raised by a family that is also Catholic. You may want your child to grow up with the same customs and traditions that you had as a child. To others a loving environment is more important, and religion does not become an issue.

I had clients, a wonderful couple, who became the "second choice" as a result of their religious denomination. It is not something that adoptive couples could foresee or for which they could prepare. Nor is it something people generally want to change. Some prospective adoptive families and birthfamilies are very committed to the idea that the baby be born from or raised in a specific denomination or religion, and that is their prerogative. I do not think you have to hide your faith under a bushel if it is an important part of your life. I always made it clear in my own personal portfolios that I have a strong faith in God, instilled in me by my mother. I did not mention denomination and was never turned down by a prospective birthmother due to my faith, nor did any expectant mother ask about my denomination.

- Is location an issue?

  If you are hoping for a fairly open adoption, then you may wish to choose a family locally. Other birthmoms think having their child so close would be harder so they opt to choose a family that is a little further away. Keep in mind that circumstances can change and people can move.

If you know you are receptive to having a fairly open adoption, this does not have to be a huge hurdle if you are shown to a prospective birthmother who is primarily looking at local couples. If you are prepared to "meet halfway," by helping her to arrange for transportation to visit the child, she may reconsider her original line of thinking. People do move; she may even need to move. It is good, if you know this is something you want, to share a willingness to work with the birthfamily to come to a plan that is doable for everyone. However, this is not something you need to do in your portfolio.

- Are the races of the prospective adoptive couple important to you?

  Some expectant moms who are giving birth to biracial babies will choose a couple with at least one member sharing the child's ethnic background so the child can learn ethnic traditions and history that might not otherwise be taught.

If you have considered adopting a child of a different ethnic background than yours, it is important to reassure prospective birthparents of the ways you plan on teaching their child the traditions and history of their roots. You may also want to mention any friends you may have with a similar heritage who will play a role in the child's life.

BirthMom Buds' tips for expectant mothers choosing an adoptive family and how they affect your portfolio

The following extracts are taken directly from the tips offered to prospective birthmothers on the BirthMom Buds website (www.birthmombuds.com). I was given special permission to use them by BirthMom Buds in hopes of helping both prospective adoptive parents and birthmothers and to foster greater understanding.

BirthMom Buds' Tips for Expectant Mothers Choosing an Adoptive Family

- Do not rush. While you may prefer to find a family during your pregnancy so you can start getting to know them before the birth of your baby, there is no rule that says they must be found and chosen before the birth of the baby. You can still choose a family afterward, so do not let an impending due date rush you into a quick decision.

Some birthmothers do wait to choose a family after the baby is born. As an adoptive family, depending on your home state, this could mean that all relinquishment papers, etc. have been signed by the time you are chosen to bring a child home. Of my three children, two came to me right after they were discharged from the hospital. While I loved being there in the hospital for my oldest child's birth there was a sense of relief with the second two that all the "t's were crossed" from the second I ever held them. Everyone's adoption story is unique—you never know what yours will be until you get there.

- Consider choosing an adoptive family that already has one or more adopted children with open adoptions. Ask to speak to their child's birthmom or birthmoms if there is more than one to see if the parents have remained consistent and fulfilled the promises they made before relinquishment.

There are definitely benefits to being a family who has known adoption. I was adopted, as were all three of my children and I think that can be a reassuring feeling for some prospective birthmothers. There is a greater perceived capacity for love and acceptance when it comes to families who have adopted before. For prospective birthparents who do not want an ongoing relationship with the adoptive family, speaking with prior birthmothers may not be as important. For those families who have adopted before and share an open and positive relationship with their prior birthfamilies, it is certainly a good option to offer that they speak. If you have a relationship with the birthmother of a child from your previous adoption, it may also be a nice addition to your portfolio to include a positive quote from her about you.

- Discuss flexibility. While post-adoption contact agreements are great, you may want to discuss leaving some room for flexibility and try to find a family that is okay with being flexible based on your needs and the child's needs. You will not know exactly how you are going to feel about being a birthmom until after the birth and relinquishment of your baby. During your pregnancy and the planning stages of your adoption plan, you may think that one visit a year is enough. But after relinquishment, you may decide that once a year is not enough and hope for more visits. Placing your baby with a family that is open to that possibility will be important.

You may also not yet know where your comfort level is. The important thing is leaving the door cracked for the prospective birthmother.

- Meet with more than one family, even if it is just for comparison. Some agencies may feel differently about you wanting to meet with more than one family, but it is your right to meet with as many families as you need or want. Even if you know one family is the right choice, we strongly suggest meeting with another family to compare.

While not all prospective birthparents will meet with prospective adoptive families prior to choosing, the majority of them will be given multiple portfolios from which to choose. One thing you share with the prospective birthfamilies is the desire to make the right match the first time.

- If at any time you begin to see red flags that this may not be the correct family for your child, do something about it. You are not obligated to any family. If you begin to feel uncomfortable, consider choosing another family.

The reality is that an expectant mother can change her mind. She can decide to place her child with another family or not follow through with the adoption plan at all, which is her perogative. While this can cause a lot of worry for prospective adoptive families, try to remember that this is not the norm. While the media likes to dwell on adoptions that fall apart, there are countless others that follow through to completion. Also remember that it is a two-way street. If for some reason you see "red flags" once you have matched, it may be you that needs to consider other options.

The questions prospective birthmothers may have for you and the answers you should make part of your portfolio

BirthMom Buds is an excellent resource not only for women who have placed children or who are considering an adoption plan, but also for prospective adoptive parents who want to answer the questions in their portfolio that prospective birthparents are looking for answers to. BirthMom Buds offers expectant mothers a suggested list of questions to ask prospective adoptive parents during their first conversation with them. As many prospective birthparents choose a family without meeting, or perhaps even speaking with, the prospective adoptive families, I think it is important that you answer many of these questions in your portfolio. Knowing the questions is helpful, only if you know the answers to how to incorporate the information into your portfolio. Under each of BirthMom Buds' questions, I have again commented with whether and how to include your answers to each question.

The following numbered questions come from "Questions to Ask" on the BirthMom Buds support group website (www.birthmombuds.com) and are used with special permission from BirthMom Buds.

ABOUT ADOPTION

1. Why do the prospective adoptive parents wish to adopt?

By all means, this is something you will include in your portfolio and will likely revisit if you have the opportunity to meet or speak with a potential birthmother. Infertility or secondary infertility is often what leads people to the path of adoption. Please read the Chapter 7 section relating to infertility prior to addressing it in your portfolio.

2. Do the adoptive parents desire an open adoption, do they want a closed adoption, or do they want something in between?

Depending on your agency or attorney guidelines, you may have to include something regarding your level of openness in your portfolio. You may find though, that as time passes you are more comfortable with the idea of a greater level of openness or contact. Because your feelings may change, it is a good idea, if you do include an answer to this question, not to include a "laundry list" of wills and won'ts, but rather an openness to a level of comfort for everyone.

3. What compromises are the prospective adoptive parents willing to make?

This is something you will work out in specifics with the prospective birthmother with whom you are matched. In terms of your portfolio, you can state things to the effect that it is important to you that she is as comfortable with the decisions that are made as she possibly can be. You cannot get to the point of compromise until you truly know where both parties stand.

4. Do the prospective adoptive parents have familial and community support for their adoption decision?

This is an important question to answer in your portfolio. Potential birthparents want to know that their child will be loved and accepted, not just by you, but by your whole family and network of friends. Family and friends pages can be wonderful places to elaborate on the excitement those closest to you feel in anticipation of your adopting.

5. Do they belong to or will they join any adoption support or play groups in their area?

If this is something that is important to you and you have already looked into it, feel free to include it in your portfolio. If not, do not rush to include something. If you have an interest in getting more information, take the time to do that, and, if it is really important to the prospective birthmother and at some point she asks, you will have the answers you need to speak honestly and intelligently on the subject.

6. Have they had any education about issues some adoptees may face growing up?

It is certainly helpful to know the challenges you may face with any child you raise, be they a biological child or a child that came to you by adoption. There are things you will want to think about, such as the possible feelings of abandonment at some point by the child you are chosen to raise. Know also that, just as not all teenagers will have drinking problems, not all adopted children will have these issues either. I am an adoptee, and when I was in junior high school I went through a very curious stage and snooped in my mom's filing cabinet in search of something I did not already know about my adoption. My mom had always been very honest with me, and I do not ever remember a time I did not know that I was adopted. I also do not remember a time that I did not feel loved or supported. I think that is the element that you take from this question and elaborate on in your portfolio: the boundless love and support you will give their child throughout his or her life.

7. Are they willing to give you the type of contact you want after the birth and relinquishment of the baby? This may include visits, pictures, videos, letters, a combination of those, or other things not on this list.

Again, this is something you can discuss in greater detail with the expectant mother with whom you are matched. It is something you will want to think about. When I began the adoption process, I was open to sending letters and pictures, but I came to find that our son's birthmother preferred to receive nothing. This is not because she did not care, but because she thought that would make it all the more difficult for her. As it turns out, none of my children's birthmothers ended up wanting any kind of further contact or letters and pictures. Do not assume now that all birthparents want to be an ongoing part of your life or that you won't want to be a part of theirs.

8.   When and how do they intend to explain adoption to a child?

It is a matter of personal preference as to whether you want to include this information in your portfolio. If you are pursuing an adoption that you hope will be very open, you may want to express that if the birthmother chooses to visit with your family after placement, it could be something you all would explain together or would discuss with one another how to explain it to the child. If you are unsure or do not want further contact you may want to explain that their child will always know that their adoption was an act of love that began with his or her birthmother.

9.   How will you be referred to when addressing the child?

I have heard a number of names used for mothers who chose to carry through with their adoption plan: Birthmother, Tummy Mommy, First Mommy, Biological Mother, Natural Mother. Some people are bothered by some of the terms' implications and this is something a specific birthmother or adoptive parent may have strong feelings about. You can discuss with the birthmother with whom you match, if it is important to her, when or if you have the opportunity to speak. When I was growing up the term, "birthmother" was not one I had heard; I only knew to call my own birthmother "the woman who had me." My mom never spoke poorly about her, but rather with a gentle understanding and thankfulness. I believe this is how this question relates to your portfolio. I do not think it is important to specify by what name she will be referred to in your portfolio, but it is important to include *how* she will be spoken of. Will she be honored? Will she be spoken of with love and gratitude?

ABOUT THEIR RELATIONSHIP

1.   How did the prospective adoptive parents meet?

2.   How long did the prospective adoptive parents date before they were married?

3.   How long have the prospective adoptive parents been married?

Briefly telling the story of how you met and fell in love can be a nice way to introduce yourselves as a couple in your portfolio. If you met through friends, have known each other since childhood or met in college that can make a sweet story. You would be surprised at how many clients have sent me their information packets for text and have written that they met at a bar. There is nothing wrong with that, but the story of how you met should not be worded in that way. To say that you met while out with friends would be enough to begin your story. If the beginning of your story together is a little less endearing, you may want to focus on other elements of the day you met such as how you felt, the rest of your courtship, a special proposal.

When you give information about how long you dated or have been married it is important to use dates rather than a specific length of time, unless you plan on doing regular revisions of your portfolio. For example, if you write, "We have been married for 10½ years," that immediately dates your portfolio. It would be better for you to put, "We have been married since 2002." For more about what to include in your About Us text, see Chapter 6 Writing Your Text and Preparing for Layout.

> 4. Is this a first marriage for each parent? If not, how many times have each been married previously?

This is not a topic for your portfolio. Information about prior marriages is covered in your home study and can be made available through your agency or attorney. If it is something about which your prospective birthmother is concerned, she may ask about it further. If you have children from a prior marriage this may come into play in your portfolio; otherwise there should not be a reason to include it.

> 5. What are their thoughts and feelings on what makes a strong marriage?

This is one of the most important elements of a Love or About Us page in your portfolio, but you will answer it in a much more specific way. The question to answer in your portfolio is, "What are the strengths of your marriage/relationship?" That is the question that actually applies to the life you are offering her child.

ABOUT THEIR EDUCATION AND CAREERS

> 1. Did the prospective parents receive any education after high school?

> 2. What profession is each of the prospective adoptive parents?

> 3. What are future career goals for each of the prospective adoptive parents?

These are all questions that can be answered in the text on your individual Parent One/Two pages or on an About Us page. See Chapter 6 for addition information and page samples. In general, prospective birthparents do want to see that you are financially stable and have a good level of job security. They are not asking to see your college transcripts or an IQ score; nor do they expect you to be wealthy. Most birthparents just want to know that you can in fact support a child.

ABOUT THEIR FAMILY LIFE AND HOME

1. Do the prospective adoptive parents have any children? If they do have children, are they biological, adopted, or a combination of the two?

Your children, if you have any, will absolutely be a part of your portfolio. See Chapter 6 and Chapter 7 for specific information about what to include and how to address the issue of biological children in your home, as well as page samples.

2. If adopted, what type of relationship do they have with their child's birthmom or birthmoms?

If you have adopted one or more children, you will definitely want to include their adoptions in your portfolio. If you do sustain positive contact with your child or children's birthmother(s), by all means include information about your relationship or even a quotation from her about you. If not, it is fine. Just remember, that the most important thing is to keep your adoption story a positive one.

3. Is one of the prospective adoptive parents a stay at home parent? If not, where will the child be while they are working?

As mentioned before, there are positives about whether you will be staying at home or working. If you will be working and the child will be cared for by a family member who lives nearby, that is certainly something you will want to mention. For those who will offer a stay-at-home parent, you can certainly include the activities you will enjoy sharing on a daily basis.

4. Do they own their own home? If so, what type of neighborhood is it in? Are there good schools nearby?

I always suggest that my clients include a Home page, or at the very least, if they do not have room for a whole page, that they at least give it a dedicated section in their portfolio. You will find more suggestions of what to include on the Home page in Chapter 6.

5. What is their philosophy on education?

If education is important to you, it is certainly something you can work in to your portfolio. If you are going to be a parent who will seek out the best schools and give your child the opportunity to go to college, there are numerous places where you can include that information. Perhaps it is important to you that a child has creative outlets at home, that they are read to each night, and that they have your help and support with homework. If you are truly offering something that will benefit her child, you should present it to the birthmother in your portfolio.

6. What is their parenting style? How do they discipline?

You will be asked in your home study what type of parent you are, or what type you think you will be. You will also be asked what type of discipline you will use. Your portfolio is all about the life you will offer as a parent and to that end you have already begun this discussion. When you think about raising a child, how do you see yourself teaching them? Interacting with them? Guiding them? Having fun with them? The answers to these questions will guide you as you express the style of parenting that you are hoping to share with a child. As for the subject of discipline, that will not come into play in your portfolio.

7. Are they involved in their community? If so, what type of involvement do they have?

Do you volunteer in some capacity within the community? Do you help at a local shelter or give time to a local food bank? Are you a Girl or Boy Scout Leader? Do you coach a sports team? Do you volunteer at the school of a child already in your home? Do you provide Christmas gifts for needy families on an angel tree each year? Maybe you helped start an arts center in your community or are a member of Junior Service Club or Rotary. There are countless ways a person can give of themselves; any of which could be included in your portfolio. A good place to add any of the activities you are involved in is your Prospective Parent page or section of your portfolio.

8. Do they have extended family nearby?

If you have family around the corner, or at least within close driving distance, that is great information to share in your portfolio. You will also want to add how you take advantage of having family so close by. Do you host weekend barbecues with family? Get together for Sunday dinners? Will your children go to the same schools with any cousins of the same age? If your family is farther away, that's OK; emphasize to the prospective birthmother how often you do make the effort to see family and how you make your time together, special, quality time. See the Family page section in Chapter 6 for more.

9. What is their relationship like with each of their families?

In terms of your portfolio, you will want to highlight the positive relationships you share with both sides of your families. Family pages, and any information you include in your letter or other pages about your family, give you the opportunity to expound on what specific family members look forward to sharing with your child. They will also convey "the total package" of love, acceptance, and involvement your family offers.

10. What do the prospective adoptive parents do for holidays? What traditions are important to them?

I love, love, love Holiday/Celebrations pages in a portfolio! They are a great place to share warm family photos and special traditions your family shares. Holiday pages can be great for those who do not have a lot of pictures for the other pages in their portfolio, because most people take pictures during holiday gatherings. If you have not taken a lot of pictures, there are bound to be other family members who have, and you can borrow theirs. When we create our adoption portfolios we are always on the lookout for things that conjure "warm, fuzzy" feelings and the Holiday/Celebrations pages have it! See the Chapter 6 section on Holiday/Celebrations pages for more information and page samples.

ABOUT THEIR RELIGION

1. What religion or faith do the prospective adoptive parents practice?

2. How big of a role does faith play in their lives?

3. Do the prospective adoptive parents regularly attend a church? If so, what is their involvement in church?

While I do not suggest talking politics, you can talk religion in your portfolio. You do not have to be specific about your denomination, but if religion plays a part in your life, you do not have to be afraid to include it. I included the role my faith has played in my life in all three of my portfolios and it did not hinder me whatsoever. It is important to be yourself, while accepting that many of the specifics of your life will appeal to some prospective birthmothers and not to others, and religion is no different.

Making promises to birthparents

One of the most important things you will want to consider is the commitments you make as you write your text for your portfolio and as you begin contact with prospective birthparents. The promises and commitments you make in your portfolio and beyond should be taken very seriously. Nothing you say in your portfolio should be taken lightly, especially plans for contact with the birthfamily. No one knows this better than a birthmother. Coley Strickland, birthmother and co-founder of BirthMom Buds, is very clear about what happens when an adoptive parent makes promises to a birthparent regarding contact and then breaks them later on down the line:

> It causes us (birthmothers) to question every single promise made to us about how you would raise and treat our child. It may not seem like a huge deal to you, but if you break one promise to us without explanation how do we know you are not breaking all the other promises too? If you are unsure if you can follow through with a promise you are making regarding future contact, then do not make that promise!

Not ready to make commitments about your level of openness? You may not know right now exactly how you will feel once you match with an expectant mother…once the child joins your family…a number of years down the road. That is OK. According to Coley, many birthparents don't know either.

> An expectant mom making an adoption plan has no idea how she is actually going to feel six weeks, six months, or six years post placement and may end up wanting more or less contact than she originally thought. Also as your child begins to grow up, he or she may want more or less contact than you currently have and there needs to be room and flexibility for growth and change.

Leaving some "room" in your plan can be looked at like leaving a door cracked open. You may be more open to some things once you get to know the birthfamily, once your child is born, or when he or she is at an age to take an interest in their adoption story. When we began our first adoption I was open to letters and pictures, and possible contact when my child became of age. It was surprising to me as I got to know my oldest child's birthmother how much I cared for her and how much I missed her post-birth. She told me from the beginning that it would be too hard for her to continue contact, and I was not sure if I wanted that either. It was decided that one day, if my child was of age and wanted to meet her, she would be open to that. I think it was the right choice for both of us to leave a door open for down the road. Some birthmothers may never actually follow through with later contact, but completely closing a door in life is difficult for anyone. Be careful of making definitive statements regarding future contact in your portfolio. Some prospective birthmothers may not want any future contact and others may want regular contact, and some may just not know yet. Being too definitive so early may lessen your options in the long run.

5

Get Out Your Camera Now!— Pictures ARE Important

We now have some insight into what prospective birthmothers want to know about you, but it is not always the text that answers those questions. As a matter of fact, your pictures may determine whether an expectant mother even chooses to read your portfolio. I know that, without a doubt, you have probably spent a lot of time already worrying about what you will write in your portfolio. You are probably thinking, "Where will I find the words?"—right? I want you to remember that the pictures you include in your portfolio and how you include them are just as important as what is included in your text. Finding them in what you may already have can sometimes be a stumbling block.

When a prospective birthmother picks your portfolio up from her stack, she will see your picture before she ever reads a word. What does the picture tell her? Whether a prospective birthmother ever reads a word of your portfolio or not, she should still be able to get a feel for you and your family just by looking at the photos. Even if an expectant mother reads all of your portfolio, it is one thing to tell someone you are something or you do something, but it is a whole other thing when you can show her as well. I always tell my clients that the pages do not really "come alive" until their pictures are on them. The saying that "a picture speaks a thousand words" can really be true if you choose the right ones. You have such a limited amount of space to share all you want to with this person, so do not waste it with pictures that show and tell nothing about you.

"But I have no pictures of me!"

When I am designing a portfolio for someone, more often than not I am held up because I am waiting for pictures. If you have some time before you need to begin the actual layout of your portfolio, then use this time to take pictures of everything you do and everywhere you go. Even if you end up not using three-quarters of the pictures you take, you will have a much better chance of having what you want or need when you get to writing and laying out your portfolio. This is so important, in fact, that I chose to address it here, before we get to further addressing text content, in hopes that if you are "picture poor" you will have the time to take pictures of all you do which should be included in your portfolio.

I understood much more the issue of not having pictures of myself once I was a parent. Every picture taken was either of one of my children, or one of the children and a friend or family member. Gone were the "couple" photos of our dating and newlywed days. Suddenly, every holiday or birthday album made it seem as if my husband were a single parent, as I was busy taking all of the pictures and was never in them. Another picture quandary clients run into is that oftentimes the things we do the most, we have the fewest pictures of. We regularly have "family movie nights" with our kiddos but I do not think I have one picture of that. Yet, if I were going to adopt again that would be a great addition to my portfolio. You may find yourself in a similar position and not have a month or more to take pictures as you go about your daily life. If this describes your situation, there is a fairly simple solution: staging. There is nothing wrong with staging photos if it is in fact a picture of something you really do; otherwise it's totally untruthful and not the way you want to begin a relationship with a prospective birthparent. I have had many clients who have enjoyed baking or gardening, or even playing kickball with their child, but did not have a single picture of themselves doing it. No problem. As an example, I had a client who enjoyed cooking Thanksgiving dinner for her family each year, as several of her family members chatted with her in the kitchen. Like many of us, she was too busy cooking each holiday to stop and take the pictures and none could be found amongst her family members. All is not lost in these situations—you can still tell your story through pictures. This prospective adoptive mother simply donned an apron the next weekend when family stopped by, and had someone snap a picture as she reached into the oven with an oven mitt on her hand. She was pleased and felt more confident, as she had the opportunity to look the way she wanted to, and the picture focused on the story it needed to tell. Now a prospective birthparent could look at her portfolio, see and share in something she loved doing, and appreciate her enjoyment of her family, even though originally she did not have pictures of it.

Tips for choosing and including pictures

1. *Narrowing picture choices:* When you choose your pictures try to pick a minimum of three to five pictures for every page heading. You may not use all five pictures but having all of them at the ready will give you additional options if a picture does

not edit well, or ends up not being a good fit for the page or the story you want to tell. I do not suggest you pick more than five because it can become overwhelming the more you have to choose from. When you go through the pictures initially, it is a good idea to have many possibilities from which to choose. Once you get to the actual layout, however, it can just be too much at once to have so many choices. If you follow the other tips for choosing the best pictures, your choices will also narrow themselves.

2. *Cover me wonderful:* When you choose your cover page photo, you should choose the photo that best represents you as a couple/family. The cover page is the first thing the prospective birthmother will see and may result in whether or not she proceeds further. You should not choose a photo that is taken from too far away. The viewer should be able to look into your eyes, so your photo should be close up and with no sunglasses. You do not have to do a generic side by side, head and shoulder pose. I encourage you to try some more creative poses, perhaps with props that may tell something about you. If your husband likes to play guitar and you want to try taking some cover pictures with him holding it while you sit on your front porch, go for it!

3. *Get the warm fuzzies:* Choose pictures that show you as warm, inviting and loving. I have had wonderful clients that did not realize it, but who in their initial picture choices looked aloof or attitudinal. If you are unsure of some of your picture choices, have someone more detached take a look and give you their honest opinion. Does this mean your pictures cannot be fun or show some personality? Absolutely not! I encourage you to be creative and show who you are. Just be sure your pictures are conveying what it is you really want.

4. *Pictures as storytellers:* Let your pictures tell much of your story. Most prospective birthmothers do not want to see a page full of text. Your pictures are no less important than the story you tell through your text. It is much like that first glance when you meet someone. Odds are you have some sort of feeling about the person before they ever open their mouth. If a prospective birthmother did not read a single word of what you had written, would she have a feel for you anyway? With the correct picture choices, your answer should be, "Yes!"

5. *Working hand in hand:* Choose pictures that will go along with the text that is on the page. For example, pictures with lots of family members do not go on your "How we met and fell in love" page. Unless you are showing a romantic proposal in front of your families, or are doing a page geared towards About Us

and caption the picture with something like, "We make family our 1st priority," then the picture does not belong! If you are creating a holiday page, be sure the pictures are without a doubt, *holiday* pictures.

6. *What we don't ever want to see:* Do not choose pictures that may seem negative to prospective birthmothers. Any pictures that show you or others smoking or drinking should be left out of the portfolio, unless they can be well cropped.

7. *Quality counts:* Make sure the quality of all of your pictures is good and clear. If your picture is grainy, do not use it. I often hear people in the adoption community talk about not using older photos in your portfolio. I actually think that an older picture that tells your story, as my childhood photo on the page about my own adoption did, has more of a home in a portfolio than a newer photo that is grainy and does not tell a story. Sometimes photos taken on smartphones that have a flash are of the same quality as ones taken with a traditional camera. Others are not. Whether your picture was taken with a phone or a camera, if it has large sun spots, is over-filtered or grainy and pixilated—DO NOT USE IT! Likewise, for pictures you have lifted from a social media page or a picture site like snapfish or Shutterfly. I have had some clients who have had lifted pictures turn out beautifully and others that were not worth using. If it is a great picture but the quality is grainy or blurry it is no longer a great picture choice.

8. *Including the big day:* The use of wedding pictures in adoption portfolios has been something that many adoption agencies and attorneys have discouraged. I have even had the occasion to read guidelines for portfolios which stated that the use of wedding photos may be upsetting to a potential birthmother who is not married and worries she may never be. This line of thinking never made sense to me, as the prospective adoptive parents are telling the story of themselves. In the "it may upset the expectant mother" line of thinking, there are many aspects of the life shown in the portfolio that she would find upsetting.

   I have recently had the opportunity to ask several birthmothers, including Coley Strickland, co-founder of BirthMom Buds, what they thought of wedding photos being included in portfolios and received the answers, "I like to see the wedding photos," and "They show their love from the start." When I told one of the birthmothers that some agencies and attorneys had discouraged it, she responded, "How fragile do they think we are?"

   While I would not suggest you include more than one or two wedding photos, I do think they can be a nice addition. I included one on the About Us page in my own portfolio, as it was part of our story. I do not think you should use pictures from your wedding on your family pages, as it makes it appear as though that may have been the last time you were with your family. But I definitely think wedding photos have a home if you want to use them and if it does not violate your agency or attorney guidelines.

9. *Cropping and editing are important:* Whether you are cropping by hand with scissors or on a digital scrapbooking program, care should be taken to crop photos logically and to give care to the little things, like red-eye, wherever possible. Also, if you have the capability and know-how, it is also a good idea to make "whimpy" colors more vivid in your pictures. Many of the digital scrapbooking programs can help you with this and red-eye issues.

10. *Save some information for later:* One thing I have done for my own clients, which you may choose to do for yourself, is to eliminate all house numbers, license plate numbers, and other identifying information. This is not done because none of the clients want the birthmother they hoped to eventually match with to know where they lived, but because they only wanted to share that information with the expectant mother with whom they were ultimately matched.

6

Writing Your Text and Preparing for Layout—Insight and examples by page

When I create a portfolio for my clients I put it in a logical order. The order can apply to full-page topic portfolios or those with shortened versions of multiple topics per page:

Main pages

- Cover

- Prospective Birthparent Letter

- About Us/How We Met and Fell in Love

- About Adoptive Parent 1

- About Adoptive Parent 2

- About Adoptions in the Family

- About a Child/Children Already in the Home

- Home

- Closing

Filler pages (if applicable)

- Family

- Pets

- What Makes Us/Will Make Us Great Parents

- Quotes from Family/Friends/Co-Workers

- Holiday/Celebration

- Hobbies

- Favorites

- Travel

- Other pages unique to your family

Whether your portfolio is four pages or 20 pages you will still want to have a natural flow to your content. If your portfolio is four pages, it will flow in multiple sections per page; those with longer portfolios can give each section its own page. While I have provided you with sample pages that are more stand-alone topics, the same formula can be used to intermingle related topics; they will just each be shortened. I have had the opportunity to see a number of portfolios created by other designers, as well as the clients themselves, that have been brought to me for revision. I often note that the makers of these portfolios have fallen into the temptation of cramming too much information into one space. I want you to see that you can create something less overwhelming that is more effective and unique.

In the following pages I will give a brief description of the elements that can be included to construct your text for each section you choose to include in your portfolio. I have also included some simply done sample pages. I wanted to show you pages that are doable. You will note that there are many samples created with the landscape layout. The landscape layout gives my clients the option of printing hard or softback books with their custom pages on websites like Shutterfly (www.shutterfly.com) that can later be added to create a lifebook. Portrait-style pages do not allow for this but are what is needed to create a saddlestitch bound profile, which saves on printing costs and allows it to easily be sent via the postal service to prospective birthparents. Both styles can be quite beautiful. As always, defer to any agency/attorney guidelines. Also remember, these elements can be used whether they are done as full-page topics or are included in a shorter form on a page with other topics.

Cover

Figure 6.0 Cover page with a super cute close-up

A Little Beachy kit was designed by Sarah Sullivan and is used with permission from Design House Digital. The decorative text used for the names of this darling couple was designed by, and is used with permission from, Ali Edwards (www.aliedwards.com).

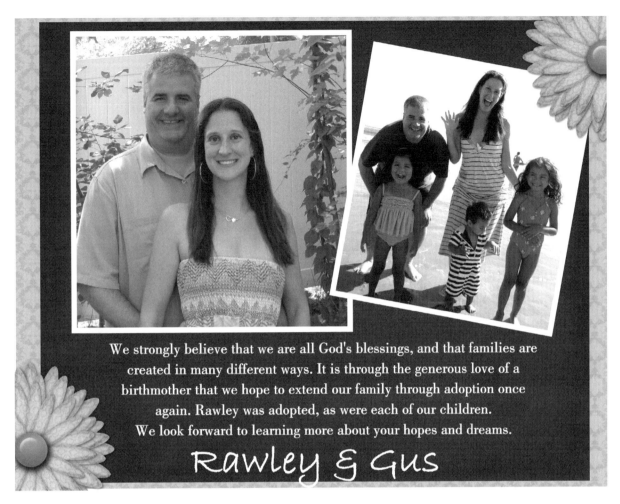

We strongly believe that we are all God's blessings, and that families are created in many different ways. It is through the generous love of a birthmother that we hope to extend our family through adoption once again. Rawley was adopted, as were each of our children. We look forward to learning more about your hopes and dreams.

Rawley & Gus

Figure 6.1 More than just "hello," this cover includes a short letter
This page was created with the Inspired kit, designed as an April House Party Collaboration from Design House Digital.

Figure 6.1, featuring a true family of multiple adoptions, includes introductory text. The portfolio itself did not include a Prospective Birthparent Letter following the Cover page, the introductory text was done in lieu of one.

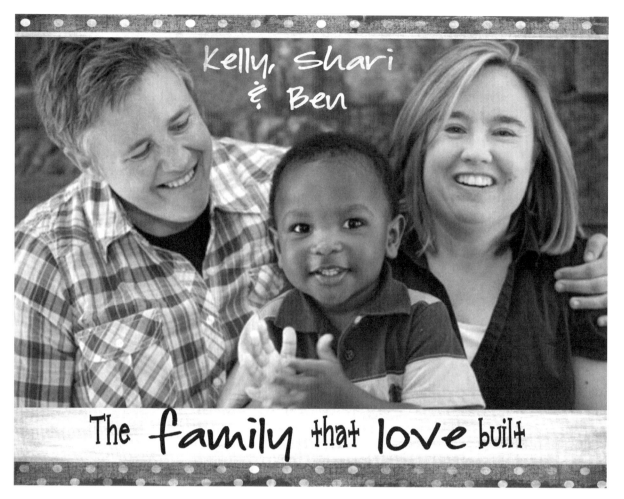

Figure 6.2 Saying more with less on this Cover page
Background from the Embrace kit, designed by Diane Rooney and used with permission from Design House Digital.

Simple says a lot on this cover page sample. Aside from the picture, their names and a background, there is also a simple statement that reflects their first adoption of their son.

Your first names will be included on your Cover page, and they may be the only text on that page. Generally, last names are not included at this point for privacy purposes. Keep in mind, you may use your portfolio online or other places where you would not want your full name "out there." You can always share your last name with the prospective birthparents, if you choose, once you are matched or meet in person.

I prefer not to put a lot of text on the Cover pages, as it is like your first handshake or "hello." You may also include a short personal or meaningful quote about love or family. Some agencies and attorneys require that the cover include what would normally be on the Prospective Birthparent Letter page. If that is the case you will want your text to be no more than two paragraphs so you may still have a good size photo.

Prospective Birthparent Letter

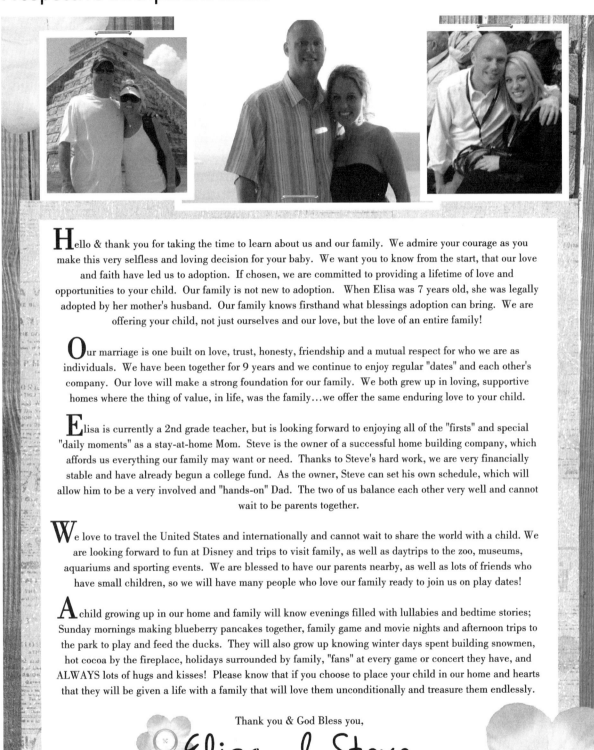

Hello & thank you for taking the time to learn about us and our family. We admire your courage as you make this very selfless and loving decision for your baby. We want you to know from the start, that our love and faith have led us to adoption. If chosen, we are committed to providing a lifetime of love and opportunities to your child. Our family is not new to adoption. When Elisa was 7 years old, she was legally adopted by her mother's husband. Our family knows firsthand what blessings adoption can bring. We are offering your child, not just ourselves and our love, but the love of an entire family!

Our marriage is one built on love, trust, honesty, friendship and a mutual respect for who we are as individuals. We have been together for 9 years and we continue to enjoy regular "dates" and each other's company. Our love will make a strong foundation for our family. We both grew up in loving, supportive homes where the thing of value, in life, was the family…we offer the same enduring love to your child.

Elisa is currently a 2nd grade teacher, but is looking forward to enjoying all of the "firsts" and special "daily moments" as a stay-at-home Mom. Steve is the owner of a successful home building company, which affords us everything our family may want or need. Thanks to Steve's hard work, we are very financially stable and have already begun a college fund. As the owner, Steve can set his own schedule, which will allow him to be a very involved and "hands-on" Dad. The two of us balance each other very well and cannot wait to be parents together.

We love to travel the United States and internationally and cannot wait to share the world with a child. We are looking forward to fun at Disney and trips to visit family, as well as daytrips to the zoo, museums, aquariums and sporting events. We are blessed to have our parents nearby, as well as lots of friends who have small children, so we will have many people who love our family ready to join us on play dates!

A child growing up in our home and family will know evenings filled with lullabies and bedtime stories; Sunday mornings making blueberry pancakes together, family game and movie nights and afternoon trips to the park to play and feed the ducks. They will also grow up knowing winter days spent building snowmen, hot cocoa by the fireplace, holidays surrounded by family, "fans" at every game or concert they have, and ALWAYS lots of hugs and kisses! Please know that if you choose to place your child in our home and hearts that they will be given a life with a family that will love them unconditionally and treasure them endlessly.

Thank you & God Bless you,

Elisa and Steve

Figure 6.3 A Letter page comes alive with pictures and elements
The A Little Beachy kit is designed by Sarah Sullivan and used with permission from Design House Digital. The decorative text used for the names was designed by, and is used with permission from, Ali Edwards (www.aliedwards.com).

You may notice that the Letter page in Figure 6.3 coordinates with one of the sample Cover pages (Figure 6.0). Your Letter page is the only page you should have this much text. While one of the pictures does include sunglasses, which I normally do not recommend because prospective birthmothers will want to be able to look you in the eye, there are two other pictures that do not. The before mentioned picture also immediately shows that this couple travels globally, which may appeal to expectant mothers as they weigh what prospective adoptive couples can offer their child.

Though this may be the first real page in your portfolio, the Letter and the Closing are always the last pages I write. Creating your portfolio is a journey in itself. You may find that it is easiest to decide what you think is most important to highlight about yourselves in the letter, once you have completed your other pages or sections.

Please promise me now that you will not use the salutation, "Dear Birthmother" or "Dear Birthparent." While there was a time when many agencies suggested this as a beginning, an expectant mother is not a birthmother until she has actually followed through with placing her child through adoption.

Many people choose to begin by thanking the reader for their consideration, which is wonderful but often becomes too lengthy and clichéd. I often like to begin with a promise. Whether it is a promise of what you will provide for her child, how she will be honored in your home or doing all you can to make her feel comfortable with her choice—the promise you make should be one you plan on keeping. If you are a family who has in some way been touched by adoption, you may want to mention that right off the bat. Not everyone has an adoption in their family so it will set you apart and, if worded properly, will show a level of unconditional love and acceptance that potential birthparents want for their children.

If you are not sure what else to include in your letter, go back and look at your other pages. What are the most important things you want the expectant mother to know about you?

- Do you have plans to stay at home with a child?

- Have you been a couple for a long time?

- Do you have lots of family nearby that will spoil a child you are blessed with?

- Are you adopted? Have you adopted a child? Are there other adoptions in your extended family?

- What are you offering their child? Love? Security? Family vacations? Sibling friendship? A college education?

- Is there something special about your home or where you live?

Other tips for your letter

- When you draft your text, never say things like, "We understand this is the most difficult choice you ever have to make." You in fact do not understand.

- Add pictures to your Letter page. The pictures keep the page from being a total block of text and allow for the letter to be used alone if the need arises.

- Do not use a tiny font. Little fonts look tedious and overwhelming. Your font should be no less than 12 point.

- For a more personal touch, sign your name by hand or with a decorative font at the end of the letter.

- Refer to the child as her child, because until she chooses to place her child, he or she is hers in every way. For example, you can say: "It is our promise to you that *your child's* life will be celebrated every day."

About Us/How We Met and Fell in Love

The couple in Figures 6.4–6.7 have About Us pages that face one another, as well as their love story from each of their points of view on separate pages. While the text portion in the love stories is a little lengthy, it was worth the risk. The couple did not leave out the loving pictures, having the love story from each of them was a personal choice they made and a good reflection of them as a couple. It was the perfect choice for the birthmother that chose them to love and raise her child!

This page is an opportunity for you to highlight the strengths you have as a couple. You may want to begin this section with the story of how the two of you met, fell in love and began your life together. Without a doubt you will want to include words that describe you as a couple and emphasize what it is about your relationship that creates a strong foundation for being parents together. This page can always be an option for quotes about one another, as well. Write about the cornerstones of your relationship: love, trust, honesty, and friendship, and then describe how you work as a team to complement each other now, and how that will make you better parenting partners in the future.

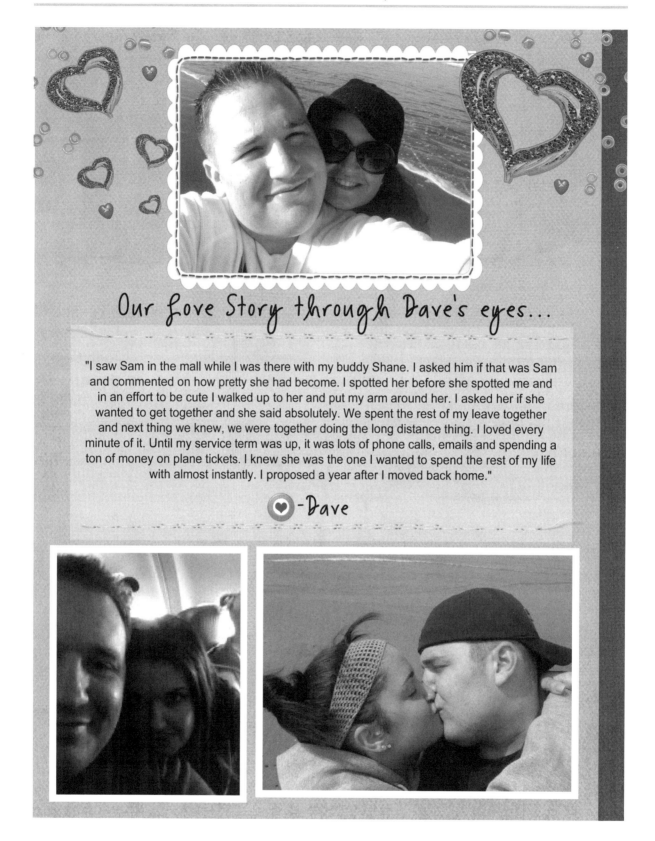

Our Love Story through Dave's eyes...

"I saw Sam in the mall while I was there with my buddy Shane. I asked him if that was Sam and commented on how pretty she had become. I spotted her before she spotted me and in an effort to be cute I walked up to her and put my arm around her. I asked her if she wanted to get together and she said absolutely. We spent the rest of my leave together and next thing we knew, we were together doing the long distance thing. I loved every minute of it. Until my service term was up, it was lots of phone calls, emails and spending a ton of money on plane tickets. I knew she was the one I wanted to spend the rest of my life with almost instantly. I proposed a year after I moved back home."

-Dave

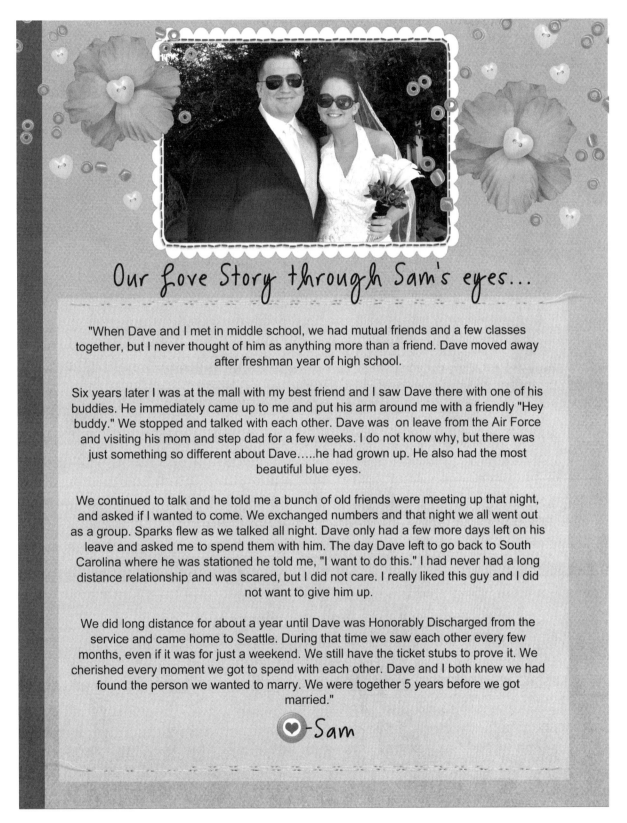

Figure 6.4 and Figure 6.5 These Love pages show another way to tell your story
These samples were created with elements from the digital kit, Valley of Love, designed
by Kate Teague, and included with permission from Design House Digital.

i love everything about you
① loving
② caring
③ fun
④ responsible
⑤ best friend

Figure 6.6 and Figure 6.7 A list, text and pictures tell all "about" this couple
These About Us page samples were created with elements from the digital kit, Key to my Heart, designed by Jen Allyson, included with permission from Design House Digital. The title font was designed by, and is used with permission from, Ali Edwards (www.aliedwards.com).

Shari is...
kind
diligent
nurturing
focused
supportive

Kelly is...
thoughtful
funny
enthusiastic
spontaneous
compassionate
adventurous

"She's here to liven things up!"

"she's the one that keeps the family going"

Figure 6.8 and Figure 6.9 A little text goes a long way on these About Us pages
This page was created with design elements from the Inspired kit, designed by Sarah
Sullivan and used with permission from Design House Digital.

These About Us page samples were created to open side by side in a portfolio. This sample has a little bit of it all: quotes, strengths, personality, and their story.

About Adoptive Parent 1 and, if applicable, About Adoptive Parent 2

Figure 6.10 and 6.11 This hopeful mom SHOWS a lot with her picture choices
The elements of these pages are from the kit, Capricious, designed by Sarah
Sullivan and used with permission from Design House Digital.

This prospective parent page sample is actually two pages, made to open side by side in a portfolio. Breaking information into small bite-sized pieces can make it easier for the reader to take in. Larger pictures also give the reader a chance to really "look you in the eye."

about *Mario*

"Mario has the biggest heart, especially when it comes to children."

~ *Laura*

occupation~
Mario enjoys financial & job security with a global leader in specialized transportation and logistics services he has been with for over 20 years

favorite childhood memories~
Summers with his sisters & raising Bantam chickens with his dad

Mario is~
a sports fan, funny, big hearted, a loving son & brother, fair, honest, a hard worker and a big kid at heart

"I hope to be a father who shows my children that unconditional love will always be given to them. Right or wrong, they will always know that I will be at their side."

~*Mario*

Figure 6.12 and Figure 6.13 Background pictures make these pages truly "individual"
The fonts used for the section titles were designed and used with
permission from Ali Edwards (www.aliedwards.com).

These two prospective parent page samples were embellished with the couple's own picture as the background. As long as you have a good quality picture you can add translucence to it and it makes the page even more your own. If you look at the font choice used for the section titles in these samples, you can see how a creative font choice can break up and define your sections.

These pages are a great opportunity, if there are two prospective adoptive parents, for each to praise the other. It is so hard to talk about oneself in the positive way that is needed for the portfolio, and it can sometimes even be perceived by the expectant parents as bragging, even if it *is* true. The best solution can be to allow for a quote or the full text to be written by the other prospective parent. You can also include reasons why your partner will make a great parent. If you happen to be single, you can use a quote written by a parent or sibling, or use all of your own text on this page.

If you have not already included information about your profession, this is also a good place to provide that information. It can be inserted either within the text or in a small text block that can break up the page a little bit. Let your personal side shine on this page by including memorable hobbies or stories and, if you so desire, some of your favorite things.

About Adoptions in the Family

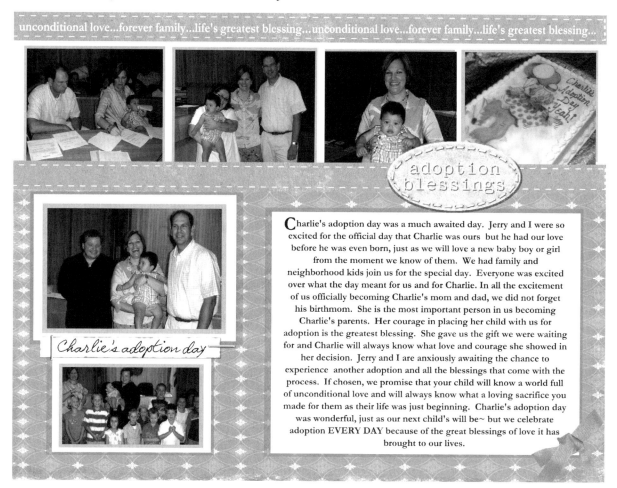

unconditional love...forever family...life's greatest blessing...unconditional love...forever family...life's greatest blessing...

adoption blessings

Charlie's adoption day was a much awaited day. Jerry and I were so excited for the official day that Charlie was ours but he had our love before he was even born, just as we will love a new baby boy or girl from the moment we know of them. We had family and neighborhood kids join us for the special day. Everyone was excited over what the day meant for us and for Charlie. In all the excitement of us officially becoming Charlie's mom and dad, we did not forget his birthmom. She is the most important person in us becoming Charlie's parents. Her courage in placing her child with us for adoption is the greatest blessing. She gave us the gift we were waiting for and Charlie will always know what love and courage she showed in her decision. Jerry and I are anxiously awaiting the chance to experience another adoption and all the blessings that come with the process. If chosen, we promise that your child will know a world full of unconditional love and will always know what a loving sacrifice you made for them as their life was just beginning. Charlie's adoption day was wonderful, just as our next child's will be~ but we celebrate adoption EVERY DAY because of the great blessings of love it has brought to our lives.

Charlie's adoption day

Figure 6.14 Adding additional comfort with an Adoption page
This page was created with the George kit, designed by Diane Rooney and used with permission from Design House Digital.

I love this adoption page most of all, because I created the original portfolio this couple used when they went on to adopt this sweet baby boy.

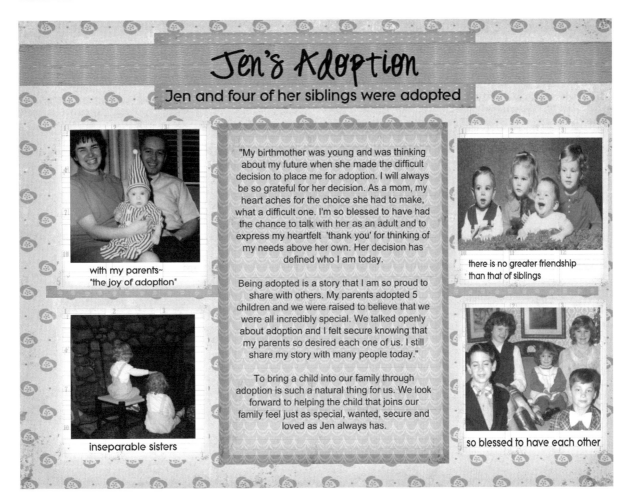

Figure 6.15 An Adoption page from a hopeful mom who was adopted herself
This page was created with papers from the digital kit, Nostalgia, designed by
Jen Allyson and used with permission from Design House Digital.

In this Adoption page sample, I love that the prospective adoptive mom and four of her siblings were adopted. In this case, pictures of them growing up made a lovely addition.

This page can include the prospective adoptive parent's own adoption, that of a child already in the home, or the adoption of other family members.

If you, as a prospective adoptive parent were adopted or if you have already adopted a child in your home, it is very important that the adoption is highlighted in your text. If you have the room, you may want to give the adoption its own dedicated page. Prospective birthparents want to know that when they choose to place their child with a family that he or she will be totally accepted and loved unconditionally. Knowing that one of the prospective parents or a prospective sibling has been adopted can bring greater comfort to the prospective birthparent. Knowing that their child will be with other people who also came to their family through adoption will help the prospective birthparent to feel that their child will not be "different." It will also help to show them that your family has already welcomed members, with open arms and hearts, through adoption. If you had a positive relationship with your child's birthmother, whether you chose to continue your relationship after your child's birth or not, that is something you will want to include on this page. If you have an ongoing relationship with your child's birthmother you could also include a quotation from her on this page.

I have also worked with a number of prospective adoptive families that include extended family members who were adopted. It is a nice addition to include those family members, noting their adoptions, or to dedicate a page to family adoptions. While it is not common, I did work with a family in which the prospective adoptive parent's mother had been a birthmother herself. That was an important addition to their letter and portfolio, as well. The more you can illustrate your family's capacity for love and their open hearts, the better!

Figure 6.16 Including other family members who were adopted

This Adoption page was created with elements from the Simple Classics No 7 Kit, designed by, and used with, permission from Katie Pertiet and Designer Digitals (www.designerdigitals.com).

About a Child/Children Already in the Home

Mark, our super fun oldest son, was born in 2002. He is in love with all things sports - especially basketball, football and baseball. He is a competitive athlete and an excellent student and really enjoys his friends - many of which live nearby and whom he has literally grown up with. On a rainy day, Mark enjoys playing with Legos, Wii or shooting hoops in our basement. When the weather is nice, Mark can be found in our backyard hunting for frogs or anything else he can capture and create a "habitat" for. He truly loves nature and all kinds of animals, especially our two dogs and cat. Mark enjoys riding his bike along the many trails that are near our house which we often do together. He is a sensitive, loving and caring individual - always putting others before himself. When he grows up he wants to be a Lawyer like his Dad.

*Figure 6.17 and Figure 6.18 If you already have kiddos,
don't hide them under a bushel—you are offering A FAMILY*
*These sample Child pages were created with the kit, All Boy, designed by Sarah
Sullivan and used with permission from Design House Digital.*

These are individual pages for a family with two children already in the home. They were created with the same kit to coordinate and ultimately be printed side by side within the portfolio. If this family had only one child, either of these pages would have been fine as a stand-alone.

When you sit down to write about the child that is already in your home, whether they came to you biologically or through adoption, it can be a concern that prospective birthparents only want a family which does not have any other children. While there are those expectant parents who think they may be doing more for their child or for an adoptive couple by placing their child with a family without children, your job is to help them see the benefits of a family which provides a sibling or multiple siblings.

When I sat down to create an adoption profile for our third adoption, it was my worry that because we had already been blessed by adoption twice *and* already had a little boy and a little girl, that we might lose our appeal with potential birthparents. I was wrong. At that time I could offer a potential birthmother, not just a mother and father for her child but an entire family as well, and that is what you need to keep in mind. We were chosen and had our son in our arms in less than a month after submitting our adoption portfolio.

As you write your text for the page about the child that is already a part of your family it is important to remember that their page, like all others, must include what your family has to offer another child.

- What can your child teach the new one?

- What does he or she enjoy doing that they can share with a sibling?

- What kind of bond can they develop as siblings?

- In what ways will your older child's temperament or personality be conducive to being an older sibling?

If you have multiple children you are already parenting and do not have the space to dedicate a page to each of them, a good option is to include all of them on one page. You can easily define the personality of each of your children with descriptive words and include a single text block describing what they have to offer the prospective birthparents' child, as I have done in Figure 6.19, showing three darling brothers.

If you have more space, you can easily add more pictures and, if you like, a larger text block. While I know the children you are already parenting *are* your world, do not lose sight of why you are writing about them. Your text should tell how the wonderful things about them apply to the type of sibling they will be to the prospective birthparents' child.

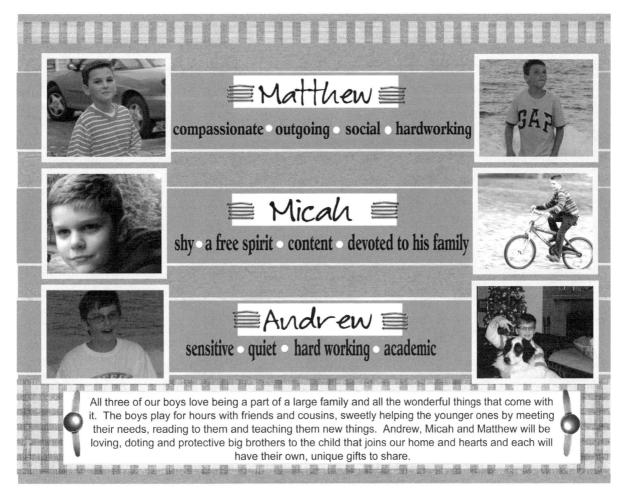

Figure 6.19 Combining multiple kiddos on one page

This page sample was created using gingham papers designed by,
and used with permission from, Katie Pertiet (designerdigitals.com).

Home

Figure 6.20 Adding things you enjoy to a Home page
This home page was created with the Embrace kit, designed by Diane Rooney
and used with permission from Design House Digital.

This client took my advice and staged a few of the pictures for her Home page. While playing in the snow and going to the park with her nieces was something she had always done, it was not something she had pictures of. If you do not already have some, I urge you to take pictures of those kinds of things. If you roast marshmallows in the backyard or enjoy family game night in your family room, by all means include photos so that the picture of your life is truly painted on your page.

Figure 6.21 Let the reader see and imagine life at your home
This Home page was created with elements from the MyMemories Suite
Scrapbooking Software, used with permission from StoryRock.

With shapes I created with the scrapbooking software I was able to design this page with no use of outside embellishment kits.

This is the basic information you will want to include on your Home page:

- Kind of home

- Room for baby/child

- Safe environment

- Family and friends nearby

- Family community

- Pool? Park? Parades?

- Will you/do you have a playroom or jungle gym?

Closing

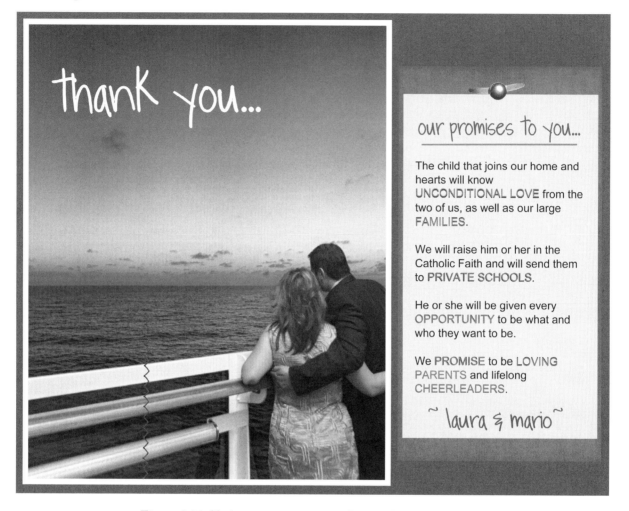

Figure 6.22 Closing page promises can leave a lasting impression
This Closing page sample was created with basic background and elements from the MyMemoriesSuite program (used with permission from StoryRock), as well as the clients' personal pictures.

As you can see, you can write your text in the form of a paragraph or as a kind of bullet-pointed list. The important part is that you leave a good, lasting impression about what you are offering the prospective birthparents' child.

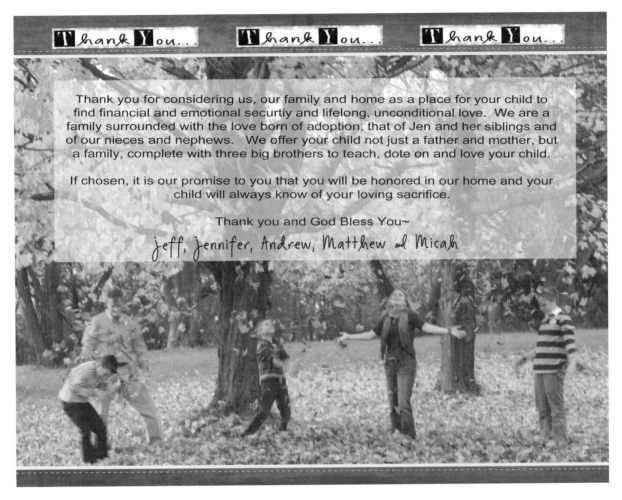

Figure 6.23 A full page family photo and heartfelt text make this Closing page a standout
This Closing page sample was created with basic background elements from the MyMemoriesSuite
program (used with permission from StoryRock), as well as the clients' personal pictures.

Where do you leave things? I highly suggest that if you have room, you include a Closing page. Having a page that will bring your portfolio full circle provides you with an opportunity to give a few last remarks and a final picture of you. This page can be many things. It can be a page of photos with a simple "Thank you" on it and your names. It can be a place to highlight some of the things you wish to offer a birthmother's child. It can also be a place to speak of your admiration for the prospective birthmother's consideration of an adoption plan. Unless you have to, do not end your portfolio on a "random page," like your Pet page. Give your portfolio the same care for a last impression that you did for your first.

Figure 6.24 Agency contact information was required for this Closing page
This page was created with elements from the April House Party Collaborative
kit and used with permission from Design House Digital.

This Closing page includes agency contact information. Some agencies request that it be placed somewhere in the portfolio, others do not.

Filler pages or sections

The following pages are considered filler pages for your portfolio. Some of these your agency or attorney may even require. I personally feel as if these pages, ot adding elements of them to other pages, can really add a lot of personality and feeling to a portfolio, and can include some of the best pictures with sometimes the least text.

- Family

- Pets

- What Makes Us/Will Make Us Great Parents

- Quotes from Family/Friends/Co-Workers

- Holiday/Celebrations

- Hobbies

- Favorites

- Travel

- Other pages unique to your family

Family

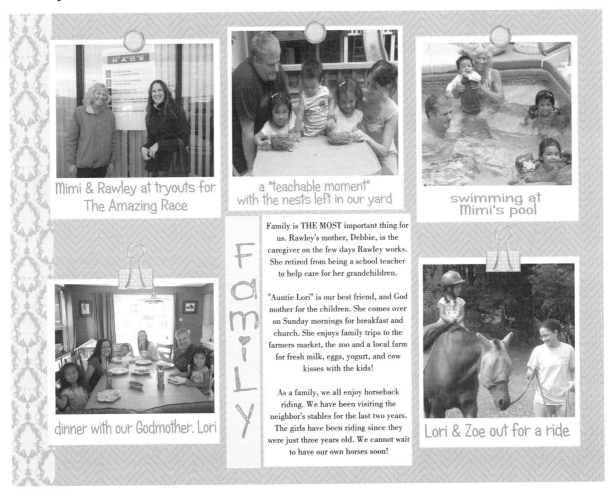

Figure 6.25 Sharing family moments on the Family page
This page was created with the April House Party Collaborative kit and
used with permission from Design House Digital.

This Family page was created for a family I had the pleasure of working with on two successful adoption portfolios.

We are a family that loves to have fun! We spend a lot of quality time together - whether its just the three of us, or with our extended family. We both come from fairly large families. Aida is the youngest of two sisters and a brother. Jose has two older brothers. We are fortunate enough to have a large family with many little cousins that all enjoy playing together.

Aida's Aunt was adopted, so we have all known such a positive, wonderful experience of adoption and the blessings it brings. Both of our families are very excited that we are pursuing adoption and have all been very supportive. They cannot wait to shower the newest member of the family with love.

Our family gets together often and the children all enjoy playing, spending time together and making memories. Holidays, birthdays and special occasions are best when spent with Grandparents, Aunts, Uncles and Cousins.

HAPPY HAPPY

Figure 6.26 and Figure 6.27 Letting pictures of this big family speak for themselves
These pages were created, to sit side by side, with elements from the digital kit, Picket Fences, designed by Jen Allyson and used with permission from Design House Digital.

While the pictures in these Family pages do not include captions, they do show a big family that is smiling and having fun. This close-knit family made use of a text block to share their family link to adoption, as well as family excitement for their adoption plan. I am happy to say the whole family is now able to love and spoil a new little boy.

Figure 6.28 A Family page unique to them
This Family page was created with the kit, Beach Collection, designed by Lisadee and
used with permission from Scrapbook Flair (www.scrapbookflair.com).

Your portfolio can be whatever you want it to be and whatever reflects your family. This particular family page uses photos of just the immediate family.

As you can see, there is only one line of text, leaving the pictures to tell the story of the fun and love their family shares. This page is all their own. I encourage you to think a little outside the box to show prospective birthparents the unique things your family offers, too!

Family pages can take on many forms. You may choose to show a number of family members and use simple captions on each, rather than a block of text. You may choose to have one or more Family pages about specific family members, such as a Grandparents page or you may make your page a Family Fun page and simply highlight fun activities you enjoy as a family.

As you write the text or captions for Family pages it is important to keep in mind that a prospective birthmother most likely is not worried with remembering or even knowing every family member's name as she reads your portfolio. You can make better use of your text space than to name all of your 15 aunts and uncles. It would be better to include a group picture of them to illustrate in one fell swoop that you have a large extended family with lots of love to share.

Through text, captions and pictures, it is most important to include the ways your family will enhance the life of the child you hope to adopt and how each family member will create warm memories with that child.

You do not have to have a lot of text. You are creating a picture for the expectant mother of the life her child would know if she were to place him or her with you. When you choose pictures for your Family page, do not waste your page with head and shoulder shots of all of your siblings—let the pictures tell their story, too. If all the sisters and nieces have their nails done together, include a picture of it. If your parents have a pool and you all come together for a weekly swim and barbeque, include a picture of it! After looking at four or more portfolios, prospective birthparents are not going to remember generic photos and a ton of names, but they will remember pictures that illustrate the feeling and experience of family that you are offering their child. Family pages can primarily do with pictures with captions and perhaps a small text block. Your captions need not list full names of family members. Rather, they should entice the reader with the experience.

Pets

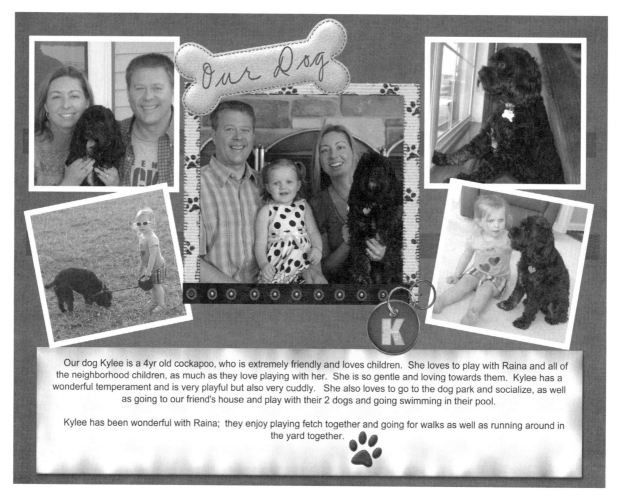

Our dog Kylee is a 4yr old cockapoo, who is extremely friendly and loves children. She loves to play with Raina and all of the neighborhood children, as much as they love playing with her. She is so gentle and loving towards them. Kylee has a wonderful temperament and is very playful but also very cuddly. She also loves to go to the dog park and socialize, as well as going to our friend's house and play with their 2 dogs and going swimming in their pool.

Kylee has been wonderful with Raina; they enjoy playing fetch together and going for walks as well as running around in the yard together.

Figure 6.29 A pup looks sweeter when shown in pictures with kids
This Pets page was created with the kit, Lucky Bum, designed by Chrissy W Design and used with permission from Two Peas in a Bucket (www.twopeasinabucket.com). The decorative cursive font was designed by, and used with permission from, Ali Edwards (www.aliedwords.com).

The pictures with their little girl, who came to them after I created their first portfolio, are not only cute, but show how patient and gentle their dog is.

Figure 6.30 A Pet page can be a must have for some families
This Pets page was created with the Dog Park kit, designed by, and used with
permission from, Katie Pertiet (www.designerdigitals.com).

Note the use of the picture with a child.

You may hear differing views on whether to include a Pets page in your portfolio or not. Some say that a number of prospective birthmothers may have had a bad experience with a particular kind of pet, so not to include them. Others will say that the prospective birthparent may have always wanted a particular kind of pet, or had one and will want her child to have one as well, so to include it. I think that if your pets are a huge part of your life and you want to include a page about them, then do it. The point of the portfolio is to share the life you are offering a child, and if the pets are a big part of it, that is OK. There are some specific things you will want to address in a Pets page or on other pages, which include pictures of you and your pets. First, you will want to include pictures of your pets playing sweetly or in a picture with children, to show that they can be loving and trusted. Second, you will want to include positive information about your pet's temperament. For example, do you have a dog that likes to play with your nieces and nephews? Do you have a cat that will snuggle up with anyone who sits on the couch? And finally, mention the positive aspects that having your specific type of pet can have on the life of a child that is living in your home.

I know that you may truly feel your pet is part of the family. Before my husband and I had children our dogs were the closest thing in our life to children. And yes, I was even one of those people that had costumes for her dogs for Halloween. It is wonderful to have pets and your future children can learn a lot from having one but please be careful in how you express yourself about your pets and their role in the family. While it is fine to say that your pets are part of the family, please do not use terms like "our furry babies" or refer to them as "sisters" or "brothers" for the child you are hoping to be blessed with. While I know terms like this are not meant to be disrespectful, you do not want prospective birthparents to feel that you are equating their child to your pet.

Great Parents

Figure 6.31 Several topics come together to show what makes this couple GREAT
This sample was created with elements from the digital kit, All Boy, designed by Sarah Sullivan, and used with permission from Design House Digital. The decorative cursive font was designed by, and used with permission from, Ali Edwards (www.aliedwards.com).

The couple in Figure 6.31 just happen to be great parents already and the page gave us room to also add family activities they enjoy.

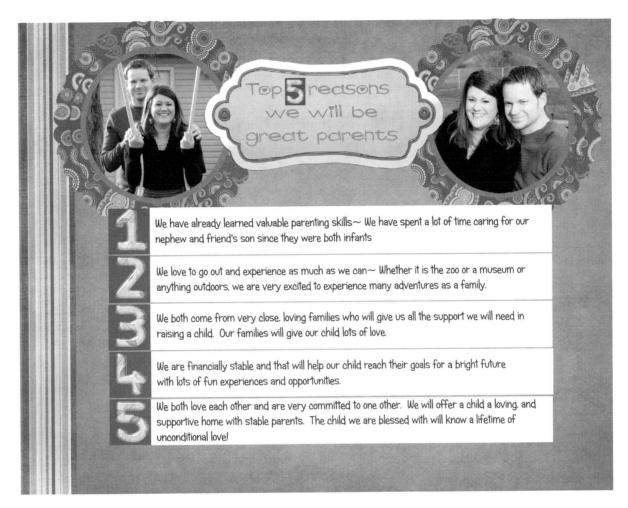

Figure 6.32 GREAT PARENTS put pictures on their pages
This Great Parents page was created with the Phoebe kit, designed by Angie Hinksman and used with permission from Design House Digital.

A prospective birthmother thought the couple in Figure 6.32 would be great parents too and they are now parents to a son!

I think that a "What will make us great parents" page can be a fun page that, without a lot of text, lists things about you that you think will make you a better parent. The lists I have seen for these pages have been night and day different, but they all played a positive role in telling the story of the kind of parents the couples wanted to be to the children they were blessed with. If you are already parenting, then this page can be a testament to who you already are as parents and what makes you great!

Quotes

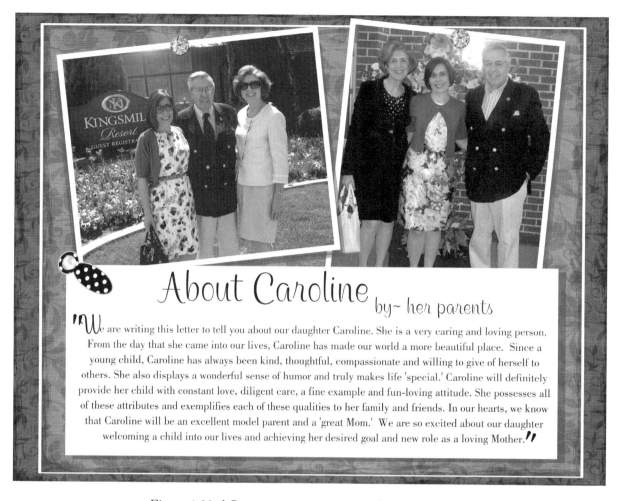

Figure 6.33 A Quote page may even come from your parents
This Quotes page was created with the kit, Friendship Collection, designed by Nayyan
and used with permission from Scrapbook Flair (www.scrapbookflair.com).

I chose to show this example because it is *not* your average Quotes page. It was created to meet the needs of a specific prospective adoptive parent. For a prospective adoptive mother who was single, having a quote from her parents was a sweet addition to her portfolio. Her parents were to be a big part of the life of the child she would adopt (and since the adoption of her son, they are). This page is a good example that your portfolio is about *you!*

A Quotes page can be so many different things. It can be quotations from each member of a couple, about each other. It can be quotations from other family or friends about you, or if you are a couple, about you as a couple. The quotes can relate to the person you are, or the kind of parent you will be, and the number of quotes may range from one to five. It is hard sometimes to talk about yourself in a positive way without feeling as if you are bragging. Letting someone else speak about your positive attributes avoids the issue of feeling like a braggart, while also seemingly adding validity to what is said, because the praise is coming from another source.

You do not have to have a stand-alone Quotes page; you can incorporate it into another page. I often have the spouse/partner write the information for the other Prospective Adoptive Parent's page and that eliminates the need for a Quotes page. At the very least you can include a one- or two-line quote from another person about you on your Parent page, or perhaps your About Us page, and you will still reap the benefits of glowing characterizations from another person.

Holiday/Celebrations

Figure 6.34 Holiday pages can bring out the warm fuzzies
The Halloween Freebie kit was designed by Jen Allyson and used with permission from Design House Digital.
The decorative text was designed by, and used with permission from, Ali Edwards (www.aliedwards.com).

This Holiday page was created with the Halloween Freebie kit. It was included to show the fun the prospective adoptive parents shared with a son's friend during the fall holidays.

It paints a picture for prospective birthparents of the memories they would share with the child they wanted to bring into their family through adoption.

Figure 6.35 Let the reader SEE what makes your family unique with pictures of your traditions
This page was created with papers from the Monkey Fun paper kit, designed by
Sarah Sullivan and used with permission from Design House Digital.

This sample page incorporates holidays into other things their family does together. It shows another way to approach holidays with a Traditions page.

Figure 6.36 What do you CELEBRATE? It can make a great addition
This Celebrations page was created with the digital kit, Birthday Collection, designed by
Sooze and used with permission from Scrapbook Flair (www.scrapbookflair.com).

This family, who now celebrate with the son they adopted, included their desire to celebrate adoption days, birthdays and every day with the child that would join their family.

As I mentioned before, Holiday pages are some of my personal favorites! Even those people who rarely take pictures, either take them during their holidays or someone in their family does. This means you should have pictures for at least one Holiday page (if you want to include one). Do we want a bunch of pictures of you and 30 cousins standing in front of the Christmas tree? No, but one would be OK—it would tell the part of the story, that you have a LARGE extended family. Text on these pages does not have to be lengthy. You can use captions under specific photos to explain specific traditions, you can use a small text box or you can make the explanation part of your embellishment. What does your family do to celebrate the holidays? Do you exchange joke gifts with your siblings? Leave a real boot out for St. Nick? Have a cookie baking day with your grandmother and mother? Have 20 people over for Thanksgiving? Dress up your dogs for Halloween? SHOW your story with pictures as much as you can. Holiday pages can really be memorable and evoke warm fuzzies when the pictures tell a good story. Don't have room for a Holiday page? Include holiday pictures that tell the story on your Family page, adding a caption explaining the fun of the family tradition and how you would include a child.

Hobbies

While you may not want to include a dedicated Hobbies page, prospective birthmothers will want to see how you enjoy spending your time, and more importantly, how you will include a child in it. Some of the places that I like to include hobby pictures or information is on the About Us page if it is a shared hobby between you and your partner or on your individual page. If you say on your About Us page how much you enjoy biking together on Saturdays and stopping for a picnic—SHOW it with a picture on that page as well and use the caption area to express how much you look forward to enjoying that ritual as a family. If you love gardening, put a picture of you working in the garden on your individual page with a caption explaining how much you look forward to seeing a little one digging in the dirt. The hobbies are the perfect illustration that it does not have to be a full page, but can still be a strong element in your portfolio.

Favorites

I am not crazy about Favorites pages, as they can quickly become trivial lists of information that are taking up valuable real-estate you could use for information that is more important to prospective birthparents. But I do occasionally see Favorites pages as a requirement for portfolios for some agencies. Do I think a prospective birthparent is going to choose you because you share a love for the same kind of candy bar? Likely, not. If it is a requirement from your agency or attorney to create a stand-alone Favorites page it can be done as a list, but I would certainly add at least one picture to the page. If it is not a requirement or if there are a few things you do want to add, feel free to include them on your Prospective Adoptive Parent page. See Figure 6.10, in the text for that section.

Figure 6.37 A Travel page is a great page to paint a picture of future opportunities
This Travel page was created with the Going Away Kit, designed by Katie Pertiet
and used with her permission. Pertiet's kits can be found at www.designerdigitals.com.

Travel

If you love to travel, either in your home country or abroad, and want to continue that tradition as your family grows, this may be a page you'll want to include. You will likely want to include captions under your pictures of where you were and, if needed, what you were doing. Your text will revolve around what you would like to show a child, whether it is new cultures or more about their own. Maybe you do not venture out very far but make regular trips to a local beach or lake; you can make a great page with "day trips," too. No matter what you include in your portfolio, it should be true to your life and show room for a child in it. This page is no different. Whether you use brief captions and a text block or longer captions that explain how you would include a child, the pictures and text you choose should apply to what you are offering a child.

Other pages unique to your family

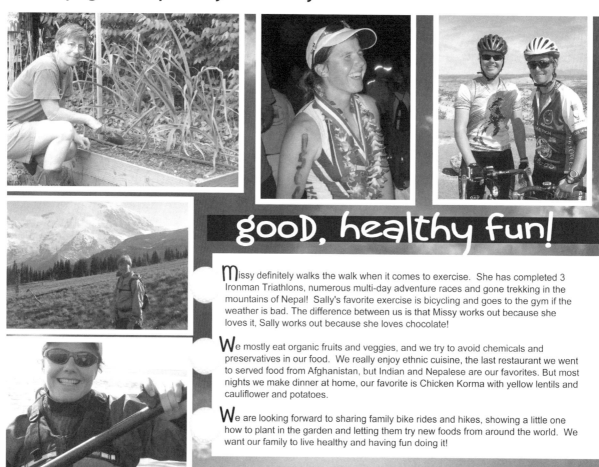

Figure 6.38 This "healthy fun" page shows what is special and unique to this family
This page was created with elements from MyMemories Suite, used with permissions from StoryRock.

Your portfolio is all about you and your family and what you have to offer a child. Do not be afraid to make your portfolio unique, as it is those special, specific things that will likely make you memorable. I am not encouraging you to take out the core ingredients that a prospective birthparent is looking for, but rather to spice it up, if you like, with things that set you apart. You can always add a page that includes things that make you, you.

Figure 6.38 is an example of this. This great couple really lives a healthy lifestyle and wanted to tell the prospective birthparents how they would share that healthful living with their child.

We look forward to helping your child develop and cultivate his or her talents, to fostering in them a love to study, grow and achieve. Without a doubt, your child will be unconditionally loved by everyone in our family.

We want you to know that your child's dreams, aspirations and well being will be our number one priority always. We promise to raise your child in a stable home surrounded by the love of parents that truly love and respect each other. Your child will also have a big brother who will love, protect and help guide him or her through life. We promise to give your child the world.

We see adoption as a miracle and we long to provide your child with unconditional love. Please know that we pray you will be given the guidance and peace you desire in making the decision that is best for you and your child. We hope to learn more about you and your hopes for your child's future.

"Prometemos que los sueños, aspiraciones y bienestar de su hijo serán lo más importante en nuestras vidas como padres. Le ayudaremos a obtener una excelente educación y cultivar sus propios talentos. Tambien tendrán la protección, amor y orientación de un hermano mayor en su vida."

If you desire, we would like to share letters, pictures and visits with you after the adoption. To get in touch with us please call AGENCY NAME at 1-800-XXX-XXXX.

Thank you.

Bill and Debra

Figure 6.39 Spanish translations made this Closing page different from the rest
This page was created with free element downloads from Scrapbook Flair (www.scrapbookflair.com).

The Closing page in Figure 6.39 was made unique by the addition of a Spanish translation. This particular couple was open to a Hispanic child and wanted to be "reader friendly" to those prospective birthparents that were Spanish speakers.

Your unique page does not have to have anything to do with healthy living or to include any translations, it should be your own. I had one couple add an Our Playlist page because music was so important to them. Whatever you choose, make it you and don't forget to explain how you would include the child you are seeking.

7

Specialty Text Issues

Infertility

Most commonly it is a fertility issue that leads a couple to adoption. Many couples have gone through months or even years of daily basal body temperature charts, hormone injections, and fertility pills that prompt crying one minute and laughing the next. Whether it was IUIs or IVFs, numerous fertility procedures are exhausting both mentally and physically and can continue to take a toll, even when you have chosen to move on to adoption. I rode the fertility treatment rollercoaster, and I was fortunate: after many hormone-altering pills and injections, when I chose to "get off that ride" my husband was still there to get off with me. All kidding aside, it can be a long and tortuous process, but you tell yourself that when you get pregnant it will all be worth it. But what if you don't? I went through almost two years on clomid (I like to call it "PMS × 100"), multiple tests of any part of my body that could have anything to do with my fertility (or lack thereof), and ultimately four IUIs before I said to my husband, "I just want a baby! Let's start the adoption process now." We had always planned on adopting at some point. As an adoptee, I wanted to adopt as well, but I had always looked at it as something I wanted to do, not something I would *have* to do if I wanted a family.

When your life has been both consumed by, and defined by, your infertility, it is hard not to go into some lengthy detail about your experiences when you get to the point of adoption and writing your portfolio. You want the expectant mother who is reading your portfolio to know that having a baby is not something you can do for yourself. You may almost want to elevate yourself above those who could have a child biologically, because the prospective birthmother may feel she is doing something even more meaningful by placing her child with you. Some potential birthmothers may feel exactly that way, but you should not recount your whole infertility story to her. I have had a number of clients who wanted to write the rough draft of their letter on their own and chose to elaborate on their infertility issues in the letter. Some dedicated a paragraph or more of their letter to the entire story of their infertility experience: tests, drugs, procedures, disappointment, grief, all of it. That is too much.

Think of things from an expectant mother's point of view. Would you want to read the following?

> We always wanted to have our own child and tried for years to get pregnant. I was on fertility drugs and we did IUIs, IVF and a number of procedures in between. Finally our doctor said that my issue of endometriosis was too bad and without a donor egg we would never get pregnant and even that was not a sure thing. That is how we found ourselves looking at adoption. We now think this was the path we were meant to take to grow our family. If you chose us for your child you would be giving us the most amazing gift.

This is very similar to things I have read in portfolios that couples were actually actively using. Let's see what is wrong with it.

1. Right away, the words OUR OWN CHILD are written. That term does not scream acceptance for adoption.

2. There is just too much personal information of the wrong kind. While you do want to be open and honest with potential birthmothers, they do not need a total rundown of what you went through physically.

3. It sounds as if fertility treatments and procedures, and even donor egg were considerations long before adoption came into play. As a matter of fact, these types of statements often make it sound like the only reason you considered adoption was because it was the LAST and ONLY option there was.

4. Think about the last line, "You would be giving US the most amazing gift." While your portfolio is about you, it is created to help the expectant mother choose a family. While there are wonderful things about you that you will share in your portfolio they will be written in a way that shows the positives of life that you are offering the child. The portfolio is about you, but not about what you will gain from it. While a potential birthmother may want to feel as if she is helping a couple to have something they would otherwise not be able to have, her first priority is choosing the family she feels will give her child the life she wants him or her to have, not to give you a gift. When it comes right down to it, you are there to be a solution to a potential birthmother's need to find a home she feels best suited for her child, not for her to be a solution to your problem of infertility.

What you can do:

1. Find the positives in your experience. Share what you went through emotionally, as it relates to your strength as a couple. How have you found strength in your partner? How has it brought you closer together? Explain how it reinforced the idea that ultimately it was having a family that mattered. Share how it could possibly make you a better parent.

2. Share your true excitement about being an adoptive parent and all that you have to offer her child. To dwell too long on the rough road of infertility takes away precious room for you to get down to what a prospective birthmother is really looking for. If you sound sad or depressed from the get-go in your letter, you may not sound like you are in a place in your life where your heart could truly be open to her child. You do not want to sound as if you are still sitting on a pity pot or that you in any way feel you have some entitlement. You want to be honest and share in your portfolio but make it a place to share excitement, joy, and the life you would like to share with a child. Many prospective birthparents do want to know what has led you to adoption but, more importantly WHY you want to adopt. The WHY is in fact the same reason you may have wanted to have a child naturally: to love them, provide them with physical and emotional security, etc. There is no need to make the answer more difficult than it has to be.

3. Put yourself in the expectant mother's shoes. She is most likely dealing with an unplanned pregnancy, or at the very least a planned one, but life has led her down a different path than she expected to take. Your problems of infertility are very different from hers. You are likely fortunate to have access to any support or resources you need to deal with the mourning the loss of the ability to carry a child yourself, but her resource is you. While repeated references to your infertility may seem to you to be saying how much you really want a child, to a potential birthmother it can read as, "we have exhausted all of our options" or "we are adopting because we have no other choice if we want a child."

If you are still mourning your loss of the ability to carry a child yourself and have not yet fully dealt with it, I suggest you look into support groups such as: RESOLVE (www.resolve.org) or the online infertility support group, Daily Strength (www.dailystrength.org/c/Infertility/support-group) to work through that specific loss before welcoming a child into your home and lives through adoption.

Same sex couple

In recent years the numbers of same sex couples who are adopting children has been on the rise. I have been very fortunate to work with a number of male and female couples who share committed, loving relationships and want nothing more than to share their lives with a child. Sadly, when I have gotten the couple's first inquiries into creating their adoption portfolios some of them have asked, "Would you be willing to work with a same sex couple?" Of course I am, and so are a number of prospective birthmothers.

As with any couple, you will, of course, want to present to the prospective birthmother your life and the life you are offering her child honestly, positively, and uniquely. You will want to show not only what makes you and your life special but also to tell of some of the things that make you the same as most other couples. Like the misconceptions that some prospective adoptive parents have about birthmothers, there can be myths that need to be exposed about lifestyles beyond the heterosexual married couple.

In your relationship you share love, strength, and friendship—these are important elements that prospective birthmothers are looking for. This is what you have in common with any other couple who is seeking adoption for the right reasons. Whether you are married or not, you are not in a fly-by-night relationship—you are in a stable, committed, long-term relationship. You are truly partners in every sense of the word and cannot wait to raise a family together. While your lifestyle may not be viewed by some as "traditional," in all likelihood you are a very traditional family, and it is helpful for you to paint a picture of the ways that you are. You may enjoy decorating the Christmas tree with extended family each year, going to all your nephews' ball games. One of you may be planning to stay home when you are blessed with a child. These are all the kinds of things an expectant mother who is looking at portfolios will need to know about you.

If you are male, that fact alone may mean you are seen in a positive light by some prospective birthmothers who would like to maintain an open relationship with the adoptive parents and their child. The fact that both prospective adoptive parents are male may actually give some prospective birthmothers the feeling that they have not truly lost their "mom" status. If you are open to an ongoing, open relationship with a birthmother it may be a good thing to highlight this with her, as initially it may not come to mind when she considers the parents with whom she would like to place her child.

If you are a female couple, you have other things you will want to add to your portfolio. One of the concerns some prospective birthmothers have about choosing female same-sex couples or single females is that their child will not have a father. This is not a hurdle you cannot cross. Much like single women who are trying to adopt, you will want to bring the element of male influence into your portfolio. Whether it is one or both of your own fathers, a brother or a great male friend who lives nearby, you will want to dedicate some space specifically to introduce him and the role he will play in the child's life. If you have numerous positive male influences in your life, that will bring love and support to the child you raise, by all means, highlight all of them. Think of some of the things that a father would do or share with a child and explain how the male or males in your life would fit the bill. For instance, if your dad was always there to listen to you and is looking forward to taking your child fishing, add a picture of him or the two of you fishing. In your text, explain how he is looking forward to taking him or her fishing, sharing long chats, and always listening. If you have a dear male friend or brother, do the same.

Single Parent

Whether it is as a result of divorce, of having been widowed, or simply of a personal life choice, the numbers of single parents who are seeking to adopt a child are growing. Despite the rise in numbers, you may have found that some agencies are not even accepting single clients. Some agencies clearly state, sometimes even on their own websites, that too many of their prospective birthparents are looking for a home for their child that includes a mother and a father. So there is not a place for prospective single parents with those agencies, but don't be discouraged. The majority of adoption agencies do accept single applicants, and I have had a number of single clients who have been chosen to love and raise a child.

Some prospective birthparents may not even realize just how open they are to the idea of placing their child with a single adoptive parent until they look at specific portfolios. A good adoption agency or attorney will encourage prospective birthparents to look at portfolios of single parents or families with children, even if they originally had not expressed an openness to those specific situations, if they believe they could in fact be a good fit for their other preferences. It is always important to show all you have to offer the expectant parents' child, but it has to be spelled out even more clearly when you are writing as a single person. Prospective birthparents may be concerned about how you will handle the responsibilities of parenthood on your own, where positive influences of the opposite sex will come from, the size of family their child would ultimately be a part of and if you can provide financially for their child.

In order to quell any apprehensions prospective birthparents may have, right off the bat, it is important to include information about:

- support you will have from family and friends

- positive influences the child will have from a family member or friend of the opposite sex

- elaborations on your job and financial security

- inclusion of any family members or close friends who live nearby, who will play an important part in the life of the child that you raise.

While most single people who are seeking to adopt are women, several adoption agencies have told me that they have had a handful of single male adoptive parents and feel it will be a growing trend over the next several years. If you are a single male who is seeking to adopt, I would suggest that you go to extra lengths to express your nurturing side. Though there are a number of men with biological children who have found themselves raising their children alone due to a divorce or having been widowed, prospective birthparents may question why a single male would venture into parenting alone by choice. Because single male adoptive parents are not the norm, you will also want to go into more detail regarding the feelings and situation that led you to your decision to adopt without a partner.

Biological children in the home

With the recent prevalence of secondary infertility, having a biological child and later looking to adoption to further grow a family is not uncommon. As I mentioned already, you walk a fine line when you write about *any* child you are already parenting, but the line becomes a little bit finer when it is a biological child. I have no doubt you can and will love the child that comes to you through adoption, as much as the child you had biologically, but I am sure you can understand that it is sometimes a worry for potential birthmothers. Do not feel that you have to ignore the elephant in the room as you approach your text; you can come right out and say that you will greet your new addition "with the same great excitement, joy, and love" as you did your biological child.

It is important that the expectant mother who looks at your portfolio knows that biology does not dictate the level of love and dedication you have for your children. In addition to expressing your capacity for love of the children you raise, either biologically or adopted, it is important to explain the additional love the expectant mother's child would also receive from the child who is currently in your home. Siblings have a special bond and you can paint a picture in your text of the memories the children will create together and the lifelong friendship they will share. Whether the child you are already parenting is biological or came to you through adoption, include in your text all of the ways your child can teach, share, and enhance the life of the prospective birthmother's child. Your main objective in the text about your child is to show all of the love and benefits that come with having a sibling, thus making it a positive, rather than a concern for the expectant mother.

Little text allowed by agency

While you may think it is difficult to come up with text for each page of your portfolio, it can be even more difficult when your agency or attorney dictates that your portfolio have very little text. I have worked with some clients whose agencies and attorneys want a letter to the prospective birthparent(s) followed by essentially a photo album. If you are in this situation you may have the same fears I had when I could only provide a letter; how will I convey all I want/need to in such little space? What will I choose to include? Will it be enough? If you can include picture pages following your letter then you are already in a much better position than I was, and I managed to be chosen several times in just a matter of months.

When you address your letter it will be much the same as any other portfolio; you will still include elements about your gratitude, the strengths of your relationship, what you have to offer a child, information about your home or community, and details that make you unique. Pictures are always important in telling your story, and this will definitely be the case here. While you cannot reiterate your important points in further text on other pages, you can drive your points home with picture choices and captions. Think of your picture pages as an extension of your letter. Ask yourself: If I had a larger letter page and could include pictures that told the story of my letter on it, what pictures would I choose? What elements would I like to include that I cannot fit in my letter? These are the pictures you will want to include on your other pages.

As with any portfolio, your agency or attorney may or may not have defined what the topics of your other pages must be. If they have, you should of course follow them. If they have not, you can make your choices just as those who have less stringent guidelines have. The main difference will be in the inclusion of information on the page. Your portfolio layout and pictures should always lend to telling your story and you can actually accomplish the inclusion of all the text you need, even if you only do it with captions.

Think about a page like your Home page. What is it you want the prospective birthparent(s) to know about your home or community? As with any Home page you will want to choose pictures that show them the life and home you are offering their child. While you may be allowed a small text block or no text block at all, you can relay the information through your captions and page heading. For example, you may have a decorative heading at the top of your page that says, "Our hearts and home are open and waiting for a child." You can easily include a picture of your home with a caption that states, "Our warm home sits on two acres in a safe, family friendly neighborhood," and include a picture of your big Sunday gatherings with a caption that reads, "Enjoying our weekly BBQ with our family who live nearby." You can also add a picture of yourself at the local ice-cream shop with a caption reading, "Saturdays mean walks on Main Street and a double scoop." Whatever home and community mean to you, you can convey it through captions and pictures, and that goes for any other topic, as well! Whether in a text block or as captions, your pictures and what you choose to write can paint a beautiful picture of the life you are offering a child.

8

What will Your Design say about You?

Why looks count

While your content is of upmost importance as you create your portfolio, do not dismiss the importance of the way it looks. Fair or not, we live in a very visual world, and your adoption portfolio will need to be visually appealing to attract prospective birthparents and put you on a level playing field. I want to help you create a portfolio that is the best and truest picture of your life and what you have to offer, and to do it in a way that draws people to pick it up. The main goal is to have a portfolio that reflects you, and truly looks, feels, and sounds like yourselves, while giving you the best possible opportunity to be noticed and chosen by an expectant mother. Think about something as simple as buying jelly at the supermarket. If you are looking at two jars of jelly that both have basically the same ingredients and you have never tried either of them, how do you decide? One jar has a plain white label with black Times New Roman text, and the other has a decorative label and is topped with red and white gingham fabric and a ribbon. My first instinct would be to pick up the one with the cuter packaging. The same can be said for portfolios. Will prospective birthparents be more likely to pick up a colorful and visually inviting portfolio or one with little to no color or embellishment?

While our samples are printed in black and white, take a look at Figure 8.0 and Figure 8.1 and see which one you would be most drawn to.

Figure 8.0 A fully embellished Cover page sample
This Cover page sample includes elements from the digital kit, Eye Candy, designed by
Angie Hinksman and used with permission from Design House Digital.

Figure 8.1 A Cover page sample with no decorative embellishment

Think about a child's picture book. If every page looked the same and the pages did not help to tell the story, would you be enticed to turn the page? To read more? In elementary school, teachers take students on a "picture walk" before reading the book, and children make their best guesses about what the book is really about. We are taught to let picture cues help us to decipher text. Prospective birthparents will do much the same with your portfolio. It is important that the pages as a whole: text, layout, and pictures are telling your story.

Checking out the competition

Your agency or attorney may give you the opportunity to look at sample portfolios that other families have created, or you may look online at any of the many agency or profile sites that include them. Obviously, you are not looking at other portfolios to copy from, as you will see many of them already sound very much alike. If you choose to look at other portfolios, it will most likely be for the purpose of seeing what prospective birthparents are already looking at. As you peruse them, make note of the ones that stand out and are truly memorable. What is it that makes them special or unique? Though important, it likely is *not* the respect they express for the prospective birthparents' choice, or the statements related to the love that they will share with the child, as these are things that nearly all portfolios include—it *is* the more personal things that stick with you. These are the things you need to think about as you begin your own portfolio.

Styles of page layout

There are several different styles you can consider as you begin your portfolio layout: the more traditional scrapbook style or the clean lines of the magazine format. Both can be created by any of the methods (by hand, digitally, or by a designer) and customized to reflect your personality. It is more a matter of preference as to which you should choose.

If your agency/attorney guidelines do not dictate how your pages should be laid out, then it is really a matter of your personal preference. I am often more drawn to the warmth and personality of the scrapbook style for myself, but there are others who seem more suited to the clean lines of the magazine style. In some cases, I find that the style is somewhere in the middle, in order to meet agency and attorney guidelines while still adding personality.

Take a look at the difference in style. Both styles include the same text information and both have been created to be very doable, even for a novice.

Scrapbook format (two landscape pages)

Figure 8.2 and Figure 8.3 Two pages that together create an About Us section
The pages were created with digital elements from the Cupid Glitterati kit, designed by Betsy Tuma and used with permission from Two Peas in a Bucket (www.twopeasinabucket.com), where Betsy's most current kits can be found.

These two About Us pages were created to coordinate and open side by side in a portfolio.

Magazine format (one portrait page)

Figure 8.1 A "stand alone" About Us page
This page was created with basic color backgrounds using MyMemories
Suite and used with permission from StoryRock.

This page was created to "stand alone" but with the magazine style it is particularly easy to create side by side pages because the elements tend to be more basic.

As you can see, they include the same text information but the look of the page is completely different. You will note that the scrapbook-style page has more embellishment and includes decorative papers, while the magazine style used solid papers and the only hint of embellishment is the decorative text. Most of my clients "know when they see it" which style they are more drawn to, and oftentimes we will even meet in the middle somewhere.

How long should my portfolio be?

First and foremost, before you begin your portfolio, be sure you are clear on exactly what your agency or attorney guidelines require. Adoption portfolios can range in length from four pages to upwards of 20 pages. Rarely do I see agencies require less than four-page portfolios anymore, and that is to your benefit. It is difficult to convey all you want to when you have only one page in which to do it. It also gives you more room for embellishments and pictures that can lend to the feel of your portfolio and also to you as prospective adoptive parents. Whatever length is required, or if there is no requirement and you can choose on your own, you want to make the best use of the space you have. A longer portfolio does not mean that you have to fill in more space with text. With the exception of your letter at the beginning of your portfolio, you should not fill more than half a portfolio page with text. A prospective birthparent wants to see you and to get a feel for you, and that is where your pictures and design choices come into play. Leave some white space in your text boxes, break up text by putting information in caption areas with your pictures, and let much of your page be visual.

To write your text, but not let it also play out in pictures, is to do yourself a disservice. Some prospective birthmothers will remember you better from what they read in your text, while others will best remember your pictures or the feeling they got from your pictures and design, making all elements important. A longer portfolio will give you more opportunity to cover all of the page topics you want to, and to do it without any crowding of your pages. When the adoption agency we used for our second and third adoptions said they required a 15–20-page portfolio, I nearly fell on the floor. Where in the world would I come up with enough to fill up that much space? I found myself at the other extreme from the one page I had to work with for our first adoption. However, once I got started, I was amazed at how quickly I filled 18 pages. When you take the time to cover all three bases on each page: pictures, text, and embellishment and do not crowd or cramp things on the page, you will be amazed at how quickly 15 to 20 pages fill up. You are not doing a research project—you are writing about you! Learning more about what kinds of information prospective birthparents want to know about you and what kinds of pictures to include should have you well on your way to filling your portfolio, whether it is two pages or 20 pages long.

9

Ways to Create Your Portfolio

There are three basic ways to create your adoption portfolio. The first is to make it by hand with scrapbooking tools and papers. The second is to use programs and elements on your computer. The third is to hire a professional adoption portfolio designer, such as myself. You will want to decide what your comfort level is with each of the options, as well as to consult any agency or attorney guidelines, before deciding how you will begin.

Scrapbook layout: create it with your own two hands

Whether you are a scrapbooker already or just do not feel comfortable enough with the computer to attempt digital design, creating your scrapbook by hand may be the way to go. I was not a scrapbooker, nor did I have an aversion to working on the computer. It was actually our adoption agency guidelines that led me to this particular design option for our first adoption. At the time, the agency we were working with required a letter that was one page, front and back. They required that numerous original photos be attached, which meant each had to be cut out by hand and glued to 100 copies of the letter. Scrapbooking by hand was my only option.

Hitting the scrapbooking aisle

Once I had made a plan of how I wanted to design my pages, I invested in some scrapbooking scissors, glue, decorative papers, and stickers. If a handmade portfolio is the direction you are moving in, do not worry that you need to special order scrapbooking supplies, as was true at one time. If you do not live near a specialty scrapbooking store or do not feel comfortable ordering things online, you can now find scrapbooking supplies at local discount retail stores and of course many hobby and craft shops carry a large selection, as well. If you would like an easily discernable selection of quality products,

Two Peas in a Bucket (www.twopeasinabucket.com) offers physical scrapbooking supplies and can easily be found under headings such as: tools, papers, stickers, and so on, making the process much less overwhelming. Two Peas in a Bucket also offers blogs and tutorials, as well as a forum where you can ask more experienced scrapbookers questions.

Going into a scrapbooking aisle can be very intimidating or overwhelming if it is not something you have done before. At a larger craft or hobby store, or if you have access to a specialty scrapbooking store, you will find row after row of papers, stickers, paper punches and hundreds of other things you may never have used. It is a good idea to take with you a list of the pages you will be including in your portfolio. Your list will help you to gauge what kind of papers and embellishments, like stickers or paper punches, you will need for each page. It is very easy to get carried away and, depending on what you choose for your portfolio, things can quickly become very expensive. While I already had numerous pairs of scrapbooking scissors, the cost of the stickers and papers I chose for the portfolio for our second adoption quickly added up to nearly $250. Many of the stickers I wanted to use required that I purchase the full package, though I only needed one or two stickers. A package of decorative stickers can cost anywhere from 99 cents to $8.00, and if you do not need the whole package that can mean a lot of money is wasted on unused product. Do-it-yourself by hand is not always the least expensive route but there are ways you can save some money. If you are not a scrapbooker, but have a friend or family member who is, ask them if you can enlist their help and borrow some of their basic tools, which will save you some headaches, and some money!

Some of the basic scrapbooking tools you will need:

- Scrapbook paper (Choose papers for each page of your portfolio. You may also want to choose coordinating papers to use as photo or text borders.)

- Scrapbooking scissors with varied edges

- Glue dots/tabs or quality glue sticks

- Stickers that go with chosen page themes (Avoid stickers and embellishments that raise very far from the page as they may not print well.)

How to plan your pages when laying out by hand

When you are creating your portfolio by hand, you will first want to make some sketches of the way you would like each page to look. If you have already chosen your pictures and written your text for the pages, the process will become much easier.

Figure 9.0 Beginning with a rough sketch

As you can see in Figure 9.0, just sketching out an idea or finding a spot on the page for each required portion of the page will give you a better idea of what else is needed.

Figure 9.1 Adding pictures and specifics to a rough page
The layout sample uses a decorative font called Baby Boston, courtesy of
Kevin and Amanda (www.kevinandamanda.com).

You will first want to copy the pictures you plan on using, as well as make a copy of your text. You can use a program like Microsoft Word to type in your text and print it out. Cut out the copies and arrange them on a piece of printer paper.

Using copies of your text and pictures, rather than the originals, gives you the opportunity to "make mistakes" and try new things as you work towards the materials and layout you most prefer. If you have not yet chosen the decorative scrapbook paper and embellishment you will use for the pages, this will give you the opportunity to see how much your page can handle.

If you do not have a lot of text and your pictures are larger, then perhaps you can choose a more decorative background, or more sticker or cutout embellishment. If you have a number of pictures or a lot of text you may want to go with a more basic design. Consider editing your text or breaking things up with smaller text blocks or bullet points for basic information. Keep in mind you will want to leave some room along the left-hand side of the page if you are going to need to do any kind of binding when you are finished. If you choose to put your pages in sleeves that go into a binder or presentation folder, you can utilize the whole page.

Figure 9.2 Adding embellishment to your rough page
The layout sample uses a decorative font called Baby Boston, courtesy of
Kevin and Amanda (www.kevinandamanda.com).

Once you have rough sketches of each page, you can begin the actual page construction. This is the fun part! This is the part of the process where you can really show your personality. From paper to font choices, you have the opportunity to give each page its own feel. You can use word art stickers for your headings, such as "Love" and "Home" or choose a fun font and print it out for decorative cutting. Once you have your text and pictures cut out, place them on the page but don't glue them on yet. Take out any sticker embellishments or other cutouts you have chosen and arrange them on the page with the pictures and text to see what looks best, and only then will you adhere all of your elements (see Figure 9.2).

You may find that what you originally had in mind doesn't actually fit and work best on the page, and that is OK. That is why there is no gluing until you have had a chance to see what it will really look like. You can always play around with new backgrounds, arrangements, and embellishments until the page looks and feels like you (see Figure 9.3).

Figure 9.3 Making a rough page prettier
This sample page contains elements from the kit, Picket Fences, designed by Jen
Allyson and used with permission from Design House Digital.

Digital layout: technology can be your best friend

The second way to create your portfolio is by using digital programs on your computer. Don't worry—you do not have to be a computer whiz to create your portfolio in this manner. It is a very forgiving way to create your layout, as everything you need is in the computer and can easily be moved around on the digital page as you work to create the vision you have in your head. In creating a digital layout from scratch, there are the same basic steps to follow, just as there are when you do it by hand: add background paper, use your photos, create photo mats or accent papers, bring in embellishments (if desired), and finish with text. You can use these steps to create your own personal style, whether it's clean and streamlined like a magazine layout or contains drop shadows and a more traditional paper feel. A drop shadow is a shadow placed on a digital element creating the illusion that the element is standing out from the background and is casting a shadow.

There are several ways that digital design simplifies the process.

- When you create pages digitally you will have less mess as your resources are confined to the computer.

- With digital construction you do not have to run to the store or wait for something to be shipped to you if you need more embellishments or papers.

- Digital design lends to instant forgiveness if you choose to move any element on the page, whereas with traditional scrapbooking paper, once you have glued something on, some real work will be involved in any changes made to the page.

- You can try numerous design options in minutes.

Resources for digital scrapbooking programs

Figure 9.4 MyMemories Suite, user-friendly screenshot
*All computer software screen grabs are courtesy of StoryRock and MyMemories Digital
Scrapbooking, MyMemories Suite Software (www.mymemories.com).*

If you are not a person who has experience with more complicated design programs like PhotoShop and others that are similar, then my suggestion is to use a digital scrapbooking program. Scrapbooking programs can range in price from roughly $15 to $50.

Some of the more basic programs you may consider are:

- MyMemories Suite (as shown here, with permissions from StoryRock)

- MemoryMixer (www.memorymixer.com)

- CraftArtist Platinum Edition (www.serif.com/graftartist)

Many of the scrapbooking programs offer the same features, however in terms of ease of use, features offered, and built-in embellishments that have some flexibility, I think MyMemories Suite highlights best what some of these programs can do!

Resources for digital elements

Before we get to the basics of digital design, we need to "shop" for one more thing. Most scrapbooking software programs have built-in page templates, but you will find that many do not really serve your purpose. You may find that the embellishments and papers included in your chosen digital scrapbooking program are not enough to personalize your pages the way you want them to. When you need more paper or embellishment options in a digital design, you can "shop" from the comfort of your own home, in your pajamas if you want to!

For additional papers, embellishments, and kits, you can simply purchase and download from an online digital scrapbooking store.

Some of my favorites are:

- Scrapbook Flair (www.scrapbookflair.com)

- Scrapvine Digital Scrapbooking (www.scrapvine.com)

- Designer Digitals (www.designerdigitals.com)

- Two Peas in a Bucket (www.twopeasinabucket.com)

Most of the sites listed require you to download a zip file that includes the elements you have chosen and purchased. Once you unzip the files and save them to a folder on your computer you will be able to access them as you create your pages on a digital scrapbooking program. Most digital scrapbook elements sites also offer free downloads too. The free items give you the chance to try out their product for quality and ease of use before you actually buy anything. The free products also give you the opportunity to play around with inserting digital elements that were not built into your scrapbooking program and give you a feel for how you can really customize your pages.

The kits and embellishments you choose to design your page really do have an impact on the feel of the page, so please take your time and find things that are appropriate to the page and how you want to be seen. Also, do not feel you have to buy a kit for every page, as some kits have enough variety that you can use them on several pages. I personally like for my core pages (Cover, Letter and Closing page) to coordinate to bring the portfolio full circle; that means, I could use one kit that I loved for all three pages.

Likewise, if you purchase a kit and then decide it is not what you need for the page, not to worry, you can likely use it for another page.

Figure 9.5 and Figure 9.6 One digital kit creates two different pages
Papers and embellishments from a kit designed by, and used
with permission from, Michelle Stein of Scrapvine (www.scrapvine.com).

Take a look at these two pages—one is a Cover page and the other a Home page. Both pages utilize the exact same papers and embellishments from the same kit.

You are not locked in to the page you purchased the kit for—you may just need to think about where else it would work. Some kits have so many varying elements that you can use them for totally different pages than those you already completed from the set.

Figure 9.7 More embellishments from the same kit give an entirely different look to the Cover page
Cover page from the same Michelle Stein kit used in Figures 9.5 and 9.6 (www.scrapvine.com).
Decorative text designed by, and used with permission from, Ali Edwards (www.aliedwards.com).

This Cover page uses the same kit that was used in Figures 9.5 and 9.6 and illustrates how pages created from one kit can be so different!

While you are already downloading, do not forget the other elements of your page. You may have also noticed that I have included decorative text in my sample pages. While I would encourage you to use a more basic font for your longer text, decorative fonts can be fun and help to break up the page. When you begin your actual design, try different fonts for titles or captions. If you find you do not have the fonts you need, Kevin and Amanda (www.kevinandamanda.com) offer many beautiful and free fonts, and you can never go wrong with designer Ali Edwards (www.aliedwards.com).

The basics of "pick and click" programs

Using digital scrapbooking software, you can create portfolio pages without ever holding a pair of decorative scissors. There are a number of products from which to choose that give you the opportunity to copy design elements, add text and photos and enable you to rotate, resize, and move around all the elements of the page. You can even change the color of elements, add texture to flat shapes, and easily switch out backgrounds to create a whole new look.

Digital scrapbooking software will also enable you to customize further your portfolio pages with text. You can add text boxes, as well as create text art using different colors, fonts, and effects. The text tools usually include a number of fonts, and if you want to go the extra mile you can get yourself some beautiful decorative text sets, like those designed by Ali Edwards, for your headings. With most scrapbooking software you can also rotate the text, add shadows, change colors, and arrange the text into a number of shapes.

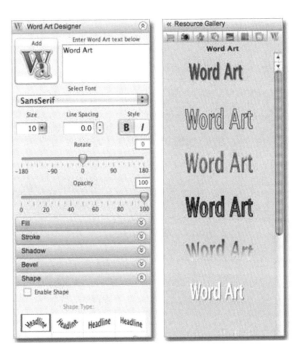

Figure 9.8 MyMemories Suite Word Art Designer
Screenshot from MyMemories Suite (www.mymemories.com), used with permission from StoryRock.

As you can see from the screenshot, just a few clicks of the mouse can take your text up a level. If you have not used a digital scrapbooking program before, it will be different, but no harder to understand, than using a desktop publishing program once you get used to it.

Most digital scrapbooking programs use "drag and drop" or "click and pick" methods for moving elements onto the page layout. Adding things like text, pictures, and embellishments can be as easy as a mouse click to the command.

Text

Scrapbooking programs will generally allow you to insert text with one click to the "add text" command, or a similar command, and then simply type it in. Some will even enable you to use the copy and paste functions simply to lift your saved text from a desktop publishing file and "paste" it to your portfolio page in the digital program.

Pictures

To add photos, you simply click the "add item from file" command or another similar "insert picture commands," choose the location where the file is stored and click your picture file name. (You can access any photo files you have saved to your computer, or you can get them from a CD or flash drive, if that is where you have saved your photos.) Also, several scrapbooking programs, including MyMemories Suite, will allow you to upload your pictures that you will be using to a "photo" section of the program. When you are ready to use them, it is as easy as "dragging and dropping" them onto the page. Some programs like, MyMemories Suite will also allow you to pre-select photos for a particular project so they are right there when you need them.

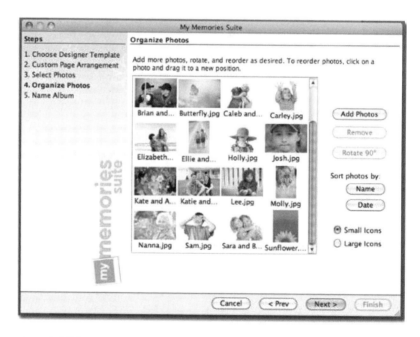

Figure 9.9 and Figure 9.10 MyMemories Suite allows easy access to your photos
These screenshots are from MyMemories Suite (www.mymemories.com)
and are used with permission from StoryRock.

MyMemories Suite illustrates how easy it can be to organize your pictures in a digital scrapbooking program before you begin your portfolio layout.

Photo editing

Once your photos are on the page you have the ability to reshape, crop, resize, and add special effects. When working with some digital scrapbooking programs, once a photo has been added, a simple right click of the mouse over the photo can also give you the options of adding borders to pictures, editing the photo by cropping or reducing red-eye, giving the photo a different shape, or adding a drop shadow.

Background papers

Background papers can be added by choosing the "add item" or "add background" tab, selecting a paper from the program library, or one from a file you have downloaded from a digital scrapbooking site, and clicking on it. In addition, on other programs such as MyMemories Suite, you will simply click on a "backgrounds bar," and, when you have made your selection from the drop down, simply "drag and drop" it onto your working page. It really is just that simple!

Embellishments

Embellishments can be added by double clicking on a gallery item already in the digital scrapbooking program or in some cases by "dragging and dropping" it. Some programs have an "add item" tab you can click in order to go to the location on your computer where you have saved elements which you downloaded from a digital scrapbooking store.

Figure 9.11 Embellishments made easy with MyMemories Suite
This screenshot is from MyMemories Suite (www.mymemories.com) and is used with permission from StoryRock.

This screenshot illustrates the simple directions and easy-to-use elements of scrapbooking programs that allow you to add embellishments.

Shapes

Most digital scrapbooking programs give you the ability to create or add custom shapes and allow you to choose the "fill" and "outline" colors. This can be a good option for creating "text box" layers onto which to place your text.

Figure 9.12 You can customize shapes in just a few clicks
This screenshot is from MyMemories Suite (www.mymemories.com) and is used with permission from StoryRock.

This screenshot illustrates the few easy "clicks" you can make to create custom shapes for your portfolio layout. It is so easy to also add shadows, rotate the shapes, change, or match colors, all of which will help you truly to customize your pages.

While scrapbooking programs may vary a little in the names of their commands and how many design options and built-in embellishments they offer, the more basic programs are very similar. Unless you have worked with a more advanced program like Photoshop before, I suggest you begin your portfolio with one of the more basic digital scrapbooking programs. These more basic scrapbooking programs were created to serve the needs of those who may not have used any type of design program before, and will garner the results you need. If you are interested in trying Photoshop, you may want to start with Photoshop Elements. Mary Shaw of Design House Digital has created a video on how to create a digital scrapbooking page using Photoshop Elements 11, which you can find at www.youtube.com/watch?v=HAFNAuPRs5E. There are also a number of digital scrapbooking tips that can be found in the digital section on the Designer Digitals website www.designerdigitals.com. Whatever program you ultimately decide to use, making the right choice for you will make the process much less frustrating in the long run.

Don't be embarrassed to use a designer

Everyone has their strengths. Not everyone feels comfortable with all aspects of the creation of their portfolio. Maybe you are an excellent writer, and, with the help of the information I have shared about what potential birthmothers are looking for within your text, and by using the workbook I have provided at the end of this book, you can create amazing imagery for your text portion. However, you may not want to broach the design aspect at all. That's all right. I have countless prospective adoptive parents come to me to create their portfolios. Whether it is because they are overwhelmed, do not have the time to devote to such an important project, or fear they do not have the knack to attempt to master something of such monumental importance, they choose not to create their portfolio. When this is the case, prospective adoptive parents may choose to use a designer.

Using a designer, if the designer does things correctly, does not mean you did not create the portfolio. The portfolio should be a reflection of you and your family. From text choices to color choices, you should still play a role in the process. The workbook I have provided at the end of this book is actually an adaptation of the workbooks I give my clients so that I can help them draft their text. I often review much of the birthmother information in this book with them when we start, as well. You are already ahead of the game, having all the knowledge you have garnered here from your experience. I do encourage you to follow this guidebook and give it a try. If you still find you are lacking in what it takes in some area, you will know where to find me (www.ourjourneytoyouadoption.com), and I would love to help you to complete what you have already started.

10

Your Final Review—Getting a Fresh Set of Eyes

Odds are that aside from work and family commitments, your time has been consumed with creating your adoption portfolio. You have stressed and worried, written and edited, put it all together on a page with layout—but you are not finished yet. Before you go to print you need to do a final edit of all punctuation and grammar. This is the perfect time to bring in another set of eyes. Even when I am creating portfolios for other couples I sometimes bring in my husband to read over what I have written before sending my clients their final proofs. It is hard when you have looked at something for so long to be truly objective. Sometimes you need a fresh pair of eyes that are not anticipating the text as you are, because you not only wrote it, but read and reread it. It is also a good idea to have someone else look at your portfolio because they can give you objective feedback. That said, you cannot ask someone who you know would only smile and nod and tell you it looks great. Ask someone that you know will be honest. When you ask a friend or family member to take a look, stress the importance of constructive, honest feedback. They do not have to be an expert to tell you if they think a page is too crowded or is not projecting who you are.

Some agencies and attorneys will also want to give you final approval before you can go to print. Do not spend extra time worrying about sending it to them. Know that whatever suggestions they may have, they are trying to help you. You can make the amendments and move on. I have consistently stressed the importance of following all guidelines you have been given by your agency or attorney, and, if you have done so, the approval process should include little to no work.

The following are general questions you should ask yourself as you make your final review of your portfolio.

- Did I follow all of the agency or attorney guidelines for my portfolio?

- Are my pictures inviting?

- Do my pictures tell a story?

- Is my text easy to read?

- Are my pages overwhelmed by text?

- Do I have spelling or grammatical errors?

- Do my pages reflect me?

- Have I included everything I wanted to?

- Have I gotten feedback from a more objective source?

- Do I feel happy and confident with my final product?

I have seen several services that will look at your adoption portfolio for $250 or more and tell you what they think is wrong with it. These services do nothing for the fee to fix it; the cost is merely to look at it and give their opinion. In most cases, clients' agencies will gladly take a look at the finished product and give feedback before the client goes to print. In some cases, approval by the agency is even required, or at the very least encouraged. If this is not something your agency does and you would like feedback on your portfolio, do not spend hundreds more to do it. I would love to see what you have created, so you can feel free to send it to me at madeleinemelcher@sbcglobal.net and I will be happy to give you feedback for free!

It is so important that you feel confident with your portfolio as you are approved to be "seen" by prospective birthparents. Once you go into the pool of other waiting families you will have control over very little. It is essential to do all you can, and feel good about it now. If you have all the approvals you need, pat yourself on the back and get to printing!

11

Printing Choices Make a Difference

So you have completed your portfolio and gotten any agency or attorney approval you need. Now it's time to go to print. Do not underestimate the difference every element of your printing choices makes. It does not matter how amazing your pictures are or how beautiful your layout is if your print quality is poor.

The importance of following agency and attorney guidelines

As with everything else in your portfolio process, it is important you check your adoption agency or attorney guidelines regarding how your portfolio should be printed and bound. Following these guidelines is important for many reasons, not least of which is that it can affect the likelihood of their sending it to prospective birthparents. If your portfolio is not printed and bound to your agency's or attorney's preferences, they may find it too heavy to send in the mail to prospective birthparents that are not local to their office. If it is a huge scrapbook album it is likely not going to make it into a manila envelope. Whether it is a simple copy with spiral binding or a hardcover book printed by an on-line service, whatever your agency or attorney is asking for you to do, *do* it! Following guidelines from the start may save you the time, money, and frustration of later having to repeat the printing process.

Choosing a printer

Several agencies with which my clients have worked have required them to use a specific printer, but for the most part agencies and attorneys leave you to choose who will print your portfolio. Your agency may tell you they would like your portfolio bound a certain way or that you need to create a hardcover book, but that still leaves you with many printing options. When I was preparing to have my own portfolios printed, I visited all the printers within a 20-mile radius of my home. I gave each a CD with a particularly colorful page from my portfolio that had plenty of pictures on it. I was amazed that some of the printers who I was convinced would produce the best quality, based on reputation and basic printing I had had done in the past, actually produced the worst quality printing of my portfolio page. My best suggestion to you is that you take a CD or flash drive with a colorful page on it to several local printers. If you have created your portfolio by hand, you will simply take your actual page to the printer for copying. Take a look at the color quality and crispness of your picture detail. Once you compare, you will have your answer.

As for printing hardcover copies of your portfolio, if you have an online source you have used before and been pleased with, by all means, use them. Personally, I am a big Shutterfly fan (www.shutterfly.com). I have always felt their products more than met my expectations and have had numerous clients use Shutterfly as well. If you choose to use another hardcover book service you will first want to be sure you can upload full pages to their format, including your original design to be used for the hard cover. It is important to be sure you have saved all of your digital pages to the highest resolution. If you use a local printer you can save to a compressed image file such as JPEG or PDF, but an online book printing service like Shutterfly will require JPEG only. Even if you have created your portfolio by hand, you will still want to have your pages scanned and saved as a PDF for your agency, as well as other marketing. If you are creating a hardback book with your handmade pages via Shutterfly or other services you will need to scan and save as a JPEG, as well, just as those who used a digital program for design would. No matter what printing source you choose, make sure the quality is wonderful, and, whatever you do, do not use your home printer!

Choosing binding

If your agency or attorney does not include the specific binding for your portfolio in their guidelines, I would suggest you ask them if they have a preference. Ask them how often they physically send out portfolios to prospective birthparents and if how they are bound may affect their ability to send them. While I like the clean finish of a hardcover book, that may not be possible depending on your requirements. If you cannot do a hardcover book but want a similar clean look, ask your printer if they offer a tape or soft book binding that will render similar results. Unless you are required to do so, please do not use those clear report covers with the slide-on piece on the side. It only harkens back to high school book reports and is not what all your hard work deserves! If you have the option of choosing for yourself, ask your printer what options are offered and which would hold up best to being handled.

The most common kinds of bindings you will find at your printer are:

- saddle stitch

- plastic comb

- plastic spiral or traditional metal

- strip

- soft book style.

Paper matters

Unless your guidelines state otherwise, or you have chosen to do a hardcover book, I would choose to print on a heavyweight cardstock. Not only does the heavier paper hold up better to lots of handling, it also feels more substantial in your hand than a standard copy paper. There is almost a subliminal effect when someone holds a higher quality paper compared to a stack of flimsier ones.

How many copies to make

I would definitely ask my agency or attorney how many copies they would suggest for their specific needs, if they have not already stated in their guidelines. Even if they only ask for one or two copies, it never hurts to ask if they may have a need for more. You never want to be in a situation where all of your copies are in the hands of potential birthparents and cannot be shown to anyone else until those are returned.

If you have a lengthier portfolio, color printing or hardcover book creation can become expensive for multiple copies. At the very least, give your agency or attorney the number of copies they have requested and then you can wait until your printer offers a sale on color copies. If you are planning on using an online source to create a hardcover book, go ahead and become a member on that site. That way when they are having a sale you will be alerted.

As you are making all of these copies, don't forget yourself! Whether it is right away, or when your printer has a sale, make a copy for yourself. Your friends and family will enjoy being a part of your journey and seeing what you have created. You will also have a wonderful keepsake for your future child. When your little blessing arrives you can add a page or pages to complete the story of your journey, all the way up to his or her arrival, transforming it into more of a lifebook.

12

Marketing Yourself, Making Use of Your Portfolio

Far and beyond, your biggest marketing tool is your adoption portfolio. Adoption portfolios are the core networking tool of agencies and a requirement for most prospective adoptive parents. Whether you are working through an agency, or an attorney, or pursuing adoption independently, your adoption portfolio will be your best tool.

Beyond its stand-alone value, you can also utilize elements you have already created for your adoption portfolio for other marketing tools to help you along your journey. By using pictures and shortened text from your portfolio, you can create the following tools with very little alteration to your page layout.

Marketing tools

Figure 12.0 Repurposed portfolio elements make up this connection card

This connection card was created using basic program elements from MyMemories Suite (www.mymemories.com) and is used with permission from StoryRock. Decorative text from Kevin and Amanda (www.kevinandamanda.com).

You can use the following tools to market yourself.

- *Connection cards/business cards:* In the case of the connection card (Figure 12.0), I just removed the text from the couple's Closing page, rearranged the pictures, and added "Hoping to Adopt" to the page. It took very little time to make those changes. The back of the card would simply need a line or two with contact information. You can "pass along" your cards because it is helpful for more people to know you are in fact trying to adopt.

- *Flyers/postcards:* A flyer or postcard could have the same front layout as your connection card, but because it would be larger you could add text snippets from your letter page of your portfolio on the back.

- *Website:* A website, either your own or your agency's or attorney's, can be very beneficial. If you are creating your own website, simply use the pictures and text you have already edited for your portfolio.

Places you can market yourself

SOCIAL NETWORKING: FACEBOOK, TWITTER

Social media is a popular way to network with other people and has also become a way for adoptive families to reach out. Social media is free and if used with caution can be an option for marketing yourself. You already have pictures and text selections from your portfolio that you can certainly use for the site you choose. Obviously, you will not want to include your last name or address in any of your postings, nor will you want to have your adoption page link to your personal page. This option has not been around long enough for there to be any real data on the outcome from couples using social media to try to connect with prospective birthparents, or people who may know of leads to them.

POSTING TO "WAITING FAMILIES" WEBSITES ONLINE

In this digital age, most adoption agencies and attorneys have "waiting families" sections on their websites. This is a no-brainer. Of course you want to be listed there! I highly encourage you to provide whatever pictures or text they will allow and to ask if your true portfolio can be posted there as well, as a PDF that can be opened by the visitors to the site. Even if you have created your portfolio by hand, you should scan your pages and save them as a PDF that you will provide to your agency or attorney. Even if it is not used on their site, it will give them quick access to your portfolio if an urgent match is required. Some agencies and attorneys prefer to allow for simply a picture (or several) and a short blurb about yourself on their site. If you are only given a short paragraph to work with, please do not waste your space saying the same things everyone else does. Use the space you are given to paint a small picture of the life you have to offer a child. If you stand out, rather than writing in the same clichés everyone else does (even if some of them are true), it will be more likely that a prospective birthparent will request your full portfolio or want to know even more about you. I have just gotten off the web where in a quick search I found countless listings just like this one, "Thank you so much for taking the time to learn more about us and for your consideration. We have so much respect for the adoption choice you are making and know it has been made with love." Aside from the fact that this blurb makes the assumption that the expectant mother has already made the choice to place her baby and presumes to "know" what she is thinking or feeling, it has also wasted valuable real estate by saying nothing that differentiated them from anyone else. When you have an entire portfolio you can give your respect and thanks—here you need to tell enough about yourself that hopefully a prospective birthmother will want to hear more. In the following examples, I have used roughly the same number of words as the clichéd example, "We are CPAs but long for the day when we can play playdoh and color with a little one and include a stroller in our evening walks." This example told a little bit about the family, as well as a few little snapshots of the future they hope to share with a child. Another example might be something like, "We love weekend bike rides, playful picnics in the park and dinners made with produce from our garden. We have travelled to five countries and 30 states together and cannot wait to show a child the world!" This example also told a lot, in a little space and painted mental pictures for the reader. *Be yourself!* Always. Whether it is in your full portfolio or a few lines used online, *be yourself!*

There are also a number of websites which now offer a home for prospective adoptive parents to post online adoption profiles for a fee. These sites offer a "fill-in-the-blank" type profile you can complete, where prospective birthparents can find you and a number of other families hoping to make a match. While the feel of the pages is somewhat generic in comparison to what we have created here, they do allow for some pictures to be added, and several offer the option of uploading your true portfolio which you created with this book to be linked to your page. Having your full portfolio available online, either through your agency, attorney, or an online profile site may give you a chance to be seen by prospective birthparents that otherwise would not see you, as well as giving them instant access to families to choose from.

If you choose to use an online profile site, just as with an agency or attorney site you can simply use text, or portions thereof, from the portfolio you have already created to fill in your information. Do not take any less care in your online profile than you did for your full portfolio. I have seen online profiles where prospective adoptive clients posted "selfies" taken with their phone as their main photo and disjointed text with multiple mistakes in their information sections. Is that how you want to be seen anywhere by prospective birthparents? Because the pages do not have your personal layout and your text will not be broken up with your pictures, be sure to add plenty of space between text paragraphs and not to add so much text that it becomes overwhelming for the reader to look at the screen. You may not be able to use all of your portfolio text on an online profile but you can certainly choose portions of it or condense what you have already created. Picture choices are important in your online profile too. Use the pictures you have already carefully chosen for your adoption portfolio. You spent all that time milling through pictures in your computer files and maybe even staging some pictures so you could show your story, use them! If you are limited as to the amount of pictures you can add to your online profile, try and use a variety from your portfolio that clearly show different aspects of your life and show a glimpse of what you are offering a child.

An online adoption profile site can be an additional way to get yourself "out" to be seen by additional prospective birthparents. If you choose to use one of these sites I recommend that you look into their safety practices, as well as what opportunities you are given to use what you have already created, such as uploading a full version of your portfolio. Again, this is an option that can certainly get you more exposure, but one I would first discuss with your agency or attorney to see their preference for what kind of contact information is posted and how to handle things, if you are in fact contacted by an expectant mother. There are still some agencies and attorneys that prefer clients not use these services at all and others that encourage their use but have a preferred site, so speak to them before you spend the money.

Word of mouth

When you hear stories of people matching with an expectant mother who was their hairdresser's niece, it may help inspire you to get out there and let people know that you are trying to adopt. Word of mouth will not cost you a thing and will become easier the more you do it. As you tell people about your journey, you can also share one of your pass-along connection cards.

Personal websites and blogs

There are so many personal adoption websites out there that I think to rely solely on a website to find a prospective birthparent would be foolish. What are the odds that it would even be found in a web search? But to use a personal website as a tool when you are already working with an agency or attorney can be very helpful. When my husband

and I started the process of our first adoption, we were working with a large, nationwide agency that spent a lot of money on marketing and had a well-trafficked website. In addition to being given the opportunity to add a picture of ourselves and a few lines about us to their "waiting families" portion of their website, we were also offered the opportunity to add a link to our own website from theirs.

Wanting to try every avenue possible to reach prospective birthmothers, I began building my website immediately after completing my required Birthparent Letters. I had never built a website before but found a site that walked me through creating one. That was over 11 years ago, and there are so many more options out there today, many of which are now free! There is no need to reinvent the wheel. I used pictures and text from our letter, just as you can from your portfolio. The combination worked. Our first birthmother called us after linking to our website from the agency site's blurb about us.

If you choose to create a website that is separate from your agency or attorney, I urge you to speak to them first and ask them about the best way to approach contact information. Could an expectant mother who is interested in you after looking at your site contact them? If expectant parents will be contacting you directly, how would your agency or attorney like you to respond?

The risks of "going public"

I suggest that if you are working with an agency or attorney, that you first consult with them relative to "going public" in the cyber world. "Going public" could mean putting yourself on a profile site, having your own website, creating a social media profile, and so on. Unfortunately, there are some, most of whom are not even expectant mothers or considering an adoption plan, who will take advantage of prospective adoptive parents and many times the odds are they are not even a potential birthmother. This does not mean you cannot or should not give it a try. You may want to filter things through your agency or attorney prior to contacting a prospective birthparent directly. I suggest that anytime you add contact information that you make a statement such as:

"For more information about our family, please contact _____ agency at 1-800-xxx-xxxx and give them our names."

If you do decide to take this route, let your agency or attorney know in advance so the potential birthmother will be connected with you. Your agency or attorney may also have rules, guidelines or tips for you to follow as you expand your search. Using the information from your portfolio to create other ways to be seen by prospective birthparents can be helpful but it has to be done in a way that will protect you.

13

Letting Go

You have gone to print, completed the steps you have chosen to market yourself with your portfolio or elements of it and your portfolio is in the hands of your agency or attorney. Now what? It is much easier said than done, but now is the time to let go a little. I have mentioned several times the importance of doing your very best, showing the things you truly have to offer a child and feeling confident in what you have done; as there is little else you will have control over. The time you spend waiting once your portfolio is handed in is the time you really have the least control. You were able to control what your portfolio said and showed, and at some point down the road you will, I hope, be able to choose whether you want to match with an expectant mother who would like to match with you. But now you wait.

I know how consuming it can be when you are waiting to match with a prospective birthmother. I personally drove my husband crazy when we were waiting and it only took a week before we had multiple contacts with prospective birthmothers. I went on to worry that what I said to expectant mothers when we spoke on the phone was wrong, and even when we matched that in some way I was going to mess things up. With so much that you can worry about, do not let your portfolio be a part of it. Does it mean that if you are shown to a number of prospective birthparents and are not chosen that you will not want to re-evaluate it? No. But when you hand it in, feel good about it and give it some time.

14

Your Dream Can Come True

I have been so fortunate to work with a number of wonderful prospective adoptive parents on their portfolios. In some instances, despite the fact that my clients come from all over the country, I have been so lucky to have the opportunity to meet them in person.

Though I love the whole process of seeing my clients go from frustrated and overwhelmed when they come to me for help to excited and hopeful once their portfolio is completed, my favorite part is the "happy endings." Many mornings I have awoken to emails from clients who say they have matched with a prospective birthmother or that the baby they have waited for has been born. Sharing in my clients' joy harkens me back to my own feelings when we were chosen for all three of our children.

When I am working with a client I often remind them that the adoption process *is* their experience of having a child. Much like being in labor, there are ups and downs, but when it is over and you hold that sweet child in your arms, nothing else matters. Your day of joy is awaiting you, do not lose sight of that. There is a child for you and I cannot wait to share in your joy, as well!

Figure 14.0 My husband Phil and I with our three blessings

15

Portfolio Workbook

Before I begin any portfolio I ask my clients to fill out my custom Portfolio Workbook. The workbook then helps me to draft their text with the information that is important. I have modified the workbook and checklist I use to create countless portfolios to help you to create yours. The checklist will help you stay organized and ensure you have what you need completed for your portfolio. Also included here is a workbook page for each of the portfolio pages I have previously given text information for. You can photocopy these if you wish. Do not feel that you have to make separate pages for each topic I have created a workbook page for; as I have mentioned before, several topics can go on one page. No matter what layout you choose, let the workbook guide you in the direction you go with each topic's text.

Basic Portfolio Information Form

Does your agency require specific guidelines for your Portfolio/Letter? Y / N (circle one)

Do you have written guidelines from an agency or attorney? Y / N (circle one)

How many pages would you like or are required to have in your portfolio? ....

Portfolio

Mark all page headings you would like/or are required to have in your portfolio.

.... Cover with a picture of you and your first names

.... Letter directly to the prospective birthmother/birthfamily

.... Story of adoption of one of the prospective adoptive parents (if you were adopted)

.... Story of the adoption of another child in your home

.... "How we met, fell in love"—The story of you as a couple

.... Adoptive parent 1
(background, childhood, occupation, hopes and dreams for your family)

.... Adoptive parent 2
(background, childhood, occupation, hopes and dreams for your family)

.... Pages about other children you already have in your home

.... Pages on other specific family members (grandparents, aunts and uncles, etc.).

List:

....

....

....

....

.... Holiday and family traditions

Check those you would like to include:

.... New Year

.... Valentine's Day

.... St. Patrick's Day

.... Easter

.... Memorial/Labor Day

.... Mother's Day

.... Father's Day

.... 4th of July

.... Halloween

.... Thanksgiving

.... Christmas

.... Hanukkah

.... Kwanzaa

.... Other: ....

.... Other: ....

.... Other: ....

.... Birthdays and celebrations

.... What makes us OR will make us great parents

.... Your home, neighborhood, town

.... Pets in your home

.... Hobbies

.... Vacations/travel

.... Family fun

.... Other: ....

....

....

.... Miscellaneous picture page with captions
(Good for including people important to you and your future child that you do not have room for/don't need a full page for or to include pictures that capture the feelings you want to share but do not have a good place anywhere else.)

.... Friends

.... Quotes about one another

.... Quotes from friends/family/co-workers

.... Closing

.... Back cover

Style you would like your pages to reflect (paper choices, etc.). This should reflect your personality:

.... traditional

.... contemporary

.... whimsical

✓

Colors you are partial to:

....

....

Colors you would like NOT to be dominant:

....

....

Printing/layout questions

Who will do your printing—local printer? online printer?

....

Will your layout be portrait or landscape?

(Remember, your layout may be defined by the type of binding/printing you choose or are required to have. For instance, a saddlestitch binding will require you to create portrait layouts that are placed side by side on an 11×17 piece of cardstock and folded. If you are required to have a Shutterfly type book in hard or softback then your pages must be landscape, as they do not offer printing in a portrait layout.)

....

Will pages be facing each other or on one side with a blank on the back?

....

....

Do you want each page to have its own feel or for all the pages to coordinate?

....

....

Agency/attorney guidelines for binding?

....   Hardcover

....   Other: ....

Portfolio page checklist

I use a sheet similar to this when I create portfolios for my clients. It gives you an at-a-glance look at what you have, what you need and what you still must do to complete your portfolio. Once you have decided what pages you will include, fill them in in the first column under the Page Name heading. As you complete the workbook section for that page, have the pictures and complete the text and layout for the page, you can mark underneath each of the relevant headings. When you are finished with a page, go ahead and give yourself a big star! If your pages require agency or attorney approval, I have included a heading for that, as well. I also like to keep track of what I have saved at the highest resolution for printing and what graphics file or scrapbooking kit I have used for each page.

Portfolio page checklist

Page Name	work bk.	pics.	text	layout	complete	approval	graphics used
1							
2							
3							
4							
5							
6							
7							
8							
9							
10							
11							
12							
13							
14							
15							
16							
17							
18							
19							
20							

Cover

Do you have several pictures to choose from for this page? Y / N (circle one)

Picture file names/location of file: ....

....

....

....

What names will you use on the Cover page or heading?
(It is suggested that you only include first names.)

....

....

Are you required to include a shortened version of the Letter page on your Cover page,
rather than a stand-alone Letter page? (Most, but not all, agencies/attorneys allow for a full
page Letter page that is separate from the Cover page.) Y / N (circle one)

Will you include a phrase or quotation on this page? Y / N (circle one)
(Do not forget to attribute quotes; use a smaller font for the attribution.)

....

....

....

....

....

Letter to the Prospective Birthparents

Much of what is in the birthmother letter will also be drawn from other parts of the portfolio, if you are doing one. For this reason, I often save this page as the last one I write. You may want to do the same.

Do you have several pictures to choose from for this page? Y / N (circle one)

Picture file names/location of file: ....
....
....
....

What would you like the prospective birthparent(s) to know about you as a couple?

....
....
....
....
....
....

As a family?

....
....
....
....
....
....

About your home/town/neighborhood?

....
....
....
....
....
....

What you have to offer their baby? (love, security, bedtime stories, lots of hugs, college education, etc.)

....

....

....

....

....

....

Other thoughts/unique things about you:

....

....

....

....

....

....

....

....

....

Prospective Adoptive Parent's own Adoption Experience

Do you have several pictures to choose from for this page? Y / N (circle one)

Picture file names/location of file: ....

....

....

....

How old were you when you were adopted? ....

Did you know your own birthmother/birthparents?

....

....

....

....

....

....

Positive thoughts or feelings you have about your own birthparents' decision to place you:

....

....

....

....

....

....

Positive thoughts and feelings you have about your own adoption experience:

....

....

....

....

....

....

How will being an adoptee yourself have a positive impact on the parent you will be?

....

....

....

....

....

Ways you will share in the adoption experience with the child that joins your family:

....

....

....

....

....

....

Other thoughts:

....

....

....

....

....

....

....

....

....

Adoption Experience with a Child Already in Your Home

Do you have several pictures to choose from for this page? Y / N (circle one)

Picture file names/location of file: ....

....

....

....

How old was your child/children when you adopted them? ....

Positive experiences specifically with your child's birthmother/birthparents:

....

....

....

....

....

....

Quotation from your child's birthmother about you:

....

....

....

....

....

....

The story of your last adoption (brief but with emotion):

....

....

....

....

....

....

....

Positive thoughts and feelings you have about the adoption experience as a whole and what you look forward to with another one:

....

....

....

....

....

....

Do you have any special ways you celebrate "adoption day"?

....

....

....

....

....

....

How do you think having multiple adopted children will help both/all feel happy and well adjusted?

....

....

....

....

....

....

....

....

....

About Us

Do you have several pictures to choose from for this page? Y / N (circle one)

Picture file names/location of file: ....

....

....

....

How did you meet?

....

....

....

Special proposal or memory?

....

....

....

Things you enjoy doing together and how you would incorporate a child:

....

....

....

....

....

....

Things you look forward to about being parents TOGETHER:

....

....

....

....

10 descriptive words about Parent 1:

....

....

....

....

10 descriptive words about Parent 2:

....

....

....

Your strengths as a couple:

....

....

....

Ways you work well as a team:

....

....

....

....

Interesting facts about you as a couple that will help you to stand out in a positive way:

....

....

....

....

....

....

....

....

(If you are not creating individual pages about you and your partner this can also be a page where you can include your occupations, etc.)

About Adoptive Parent 1

Do you have several pictures to choose from for this page? Y / N (circle one)

Picture file names/location of file: ....

....

....

....

Adoptive parent's name: ....

Favorite childhood memories:

....

....

....

....

....

....

....

....

Schools attended/degrees earned (past high school):

....

....

....

....

Occupation/about your job (including positive levels of flexibility and job security):

....

....

....

....

....

....

....

Are you planning on staying home with your child? If so, what do you look forward to? If not, what arrangements have you made to benefit your child?

....

....

....

....

....

....

Things you are looking forward to with your child and the kind of parent you hope to be:

....

....

....

....

Fun facts about yourself:

1. ....

2. ....

3. ....

4. ....

5. ....

Quote by your spouse/partner ABOUT YOU:

....

....

....

....

....

....

....

(All of this information can be worked into text written by your spouse/partner rather than including a separate, smaller quote.)

About Adoptive Parent 2

Do you have several pictures to choose from for this page? Y / N (circle one)

Picture file names/location of file: ....

....

....

....

Adoptive parent's name: ....

Favorite childhood memories:

....

....

....

....

....

....

....

....

Schools attended/degrees earned (past high school):

....

....

....

....

Occupation/about your job (including positive levels of flexibility and job security):

....

....

....

....

....

....

....

....

Are you planning on staying home with your child? If so, what do you look forward to? If not, what arrangements have you made to benefit your child?

....

....

....

....

....

....

Things you are looking forward to with your child and the kind of parent you hope to be:

....

....

....

....

Fun facts about yourself:

1. ....

2. ....

3. ....

4. ....

5. ....

Quote by your spouse/partner ABOUT YOU:

....

....

....

....

....

....

....

(All of this information can be worked into text written by your spouse/partner rather than including a separate, smaller quote.)

Other Children in the Home

(Please copy this page for multiple children.)

Do you have several pictures to choose from for this page? Y / N (circle one)

Picture file names/location of file: ....
....
....
....

Child's name: ....

Adopted? Y / N (circle one)

Child's personality:

....
....

How would he/she enhance the life of the child you are hoping to adopt?

....
....
....
....

Things he/she enjoys doing? Things they could do with the new child? Funny stories:

....
....
....
....

Things that you, as a parent(s), look forward to watching the children do together:

....
....
....
....

What qualities will make him/her a good big brother or sister?

....
....
....
....

Other Family Members/Friends

(Please copy this page for multiple family members/friends.)

Do you have several pictures to choose from for this page? Y / N (circle one)

Picture file names/location of file: ....

....

....

....

Name: ....

Relationship to you: ....

Relationship to your new child: ....

Special things about him/her or your special relationship:

....

....

....

....

Memories/activities they look forward to sharing with your new child:

....

....

....

....

Ways they will enhance the child's life:

....

....

....

....

Other thoughts:

....

....

....

....

....

General Family and Friends Picture page

(Include pictures and captions of family members and friends that are important but do not have a personal page dedicated to them.)

- These pages can accommodate four or more pictures per page.

- Captions include fun activities the person is looking forward to sharing that may also reflect what's in the picture. For example, you put a picture of "Uncle Joe" on a fishing boat and the caption will read, "Uncle Joe cannot wait to share Sundays fishing with a new little one."

Do you have pictures for this page? Y / N (circle one)

PICTURE FILE NAME	LOCATION OF FILE	CAPTION

Holidays/Special Occasions/Family Traditions: page 1

(You can include multiple events and have multiple pages on this—holidays, birthdays, adoption days, neighborhood parades, etc. There is space for two events here. Please copy for more events/holidays.)

Holiday/special occasion/event: ....

Do you have several pictures to choose from for this page? Y / N (circle one)

Picture file names/location of file: ....
....
....
....

What makes it special to your family?
....
....
....
....
....

How would you incorporate a new baby?
....
....
....
....
....
....

What makes this event/holiday/tradition unique to your family?
....
....
....
....
....
....

Holidays/Special Occasions/Family Traditions: page 2

Holiday/special occasion/event: ....

Do you have several pictures to choose from for this page? Y / N (circle one)

Picture file names/location of file: ....

....

....

....

What makes it special to your family?

....

....

....

....

....

....

How would you incorporate a new baby?

....

....

....

....

....

....

What makes this event/holiday/tradition unique to your family?

....

....

....

....

....

....

....

....

✓

Hobbies

Do you have several pictures to choose from for this page? Y / N (circle one)

Picture file names/location of file: ....

....

....

....

Adoptive parent 1's hobbies and what he/she enjoys about them:

....

....

....

....

....

Adoptive parent 2's hobbies and what he/she enjoys about them:

....

....

....

....

....

Hobbies you share:

....

....

....

....

How you will incorporate a new child into the things you enjoy doing/your hobbies:

....

....

....

....

....

Home/Neighborhood/Town

Do you have several pictures to choose from for this page? Y / N (circle one)

Picture file names/location of file: ....

....

....

....

(Please include what you feel comfortable with in this section—if you choose to do it at all. If you are not comfortable including house numbers, license plate numbers, etc., you will need to crop or blur them out of any pictures in which they appear.

Example: "We live in a neighborhood that is full of strollers and jungle gyms... We are already set up with the safest stair gates, outlet covers, fire extinguishers, and cabinet locks... Our neighborhood is part of a lovely town that still comes out for Halloween and Homecoming parades on Main Street.")

General information about your home:

....

....

....

....

....

....

....

....

What makes your home special, warm, inviting?

....

....

....

....

....

....

....

✓

Have you already made any preparations in your home for a new child? If so, what have you done? (Created a nursery? Put up a jungle gym? Made safety preparations?)

....

....

....

....

....

....

....

What makes your neighborhood/town special (parades, activities, amenities)?

....

....

....

....

....

....

....

Do you have family members or special friends who live nearby? How often will a new child see them and what will you be doing?

....

....

....

....

....

....

....

Pets

Do you have several pictures to choose from for this page? Y / N (circle one)

Picture file names/location of file: ....
....
....
....

Type: ....

Breed: ....

Temperament (e.g. sweet, gentle, playful):

....
....
....
....
....

How does your pet behave around children?

....
....
....
....
....

Do you have pictures of your pet interacting in a gentle way? ....

With you? .... with children? ....

Great Parents

Do you have several pictures to choose from for this page? Y / N (circle one)

Picture file names/location of file: ....

....

....

....

Top 10 things that will make me/us great parent(s):

1. ....

2. ....

3. ....

4. ....

5. ....

6. ....

7. ....

8. ....

9. ....

10. ....

Travel

Do you have several pictures to choose from for this page? Y / N (circle one)

PICTURE FILE NAME	LOCATION OF FILE	CAPTION

Where do you enjoy traveling?

....

....

....

Do you take vacations with extended family? If so, what makes it special?

....

....

....

....

What do you look forward to showing your child?

....

....

....

....

What do you look forward to seeing through your child's eyes for the first time?

....

....

....

....

What do you look forward to teaching him/her about other places/cultures?

....

....

....

....

Quotes from Family/Friends/Co-Workers

Do you have several pictures (if you will include any) to choose from for this page? Y / N (circle one)

Picture file names/location of file: ....

....

....

....

Specific people you will request quotations from:

Family: ....

....

....

Friends: ....

....

....

Co-workers: ....

....

....

Favorites

Do you have several pictures to choose from for this page? Y / N (circle one)

Picture file names/location of file: ....
....
....
....

FAVORITE ITEM	PARENT 1	PARENT 2

Other

As discussed in Chapter 6's section about Other pages, these pages can be anything that are unique to you and your family that are not included in the core pages of your portfolio. The couple in Figure 6.39 chose to add a page specifically about their "Healthy, fun" lifestyle. Your Other page/section can be anything that stands out about your family that you have pictures of and leaves a memorable impression.

Title: ....

Do you have several pictures to choose from for this page? Y / N (circle one)

Picture file names/location of file: ....

....

....

....

....

....

....

....

....

....

....

....

....

....

....

....

....

Closing

Do you have several pictures to choose from for this page? Y / N (circle one)

Picture file names/location of file: ....

....

....

....

Final thoughts and feelings you would like to leave the prospective birthmother/birthfamily with:

....

....

....

....

....

....

....

....

....

....

....

....

....

....